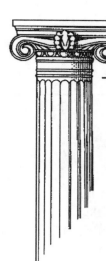

Foundations for
WRITING
Book 2
Grades 3–8

by Charlotte Slack

ecs

Printed in the U.S.A.

Editor: Lori Mammen
Page Layout & Graphics: Lisa Avitia and Julie Gumm
Cover/Book Design: Educational Media Services

These popular series of books are available from ECS Learning Systems, Inc.

Activity Books	Gr. K-12	11 Titles
Booklinks to American and World History	Gr. 4-8	12 Titles
The Bright Blue Thinking Books	Gr. 1-6	3 Titles
Building Language Power	Gr. 4-9	3 Titles
EnviroLearn™	Gr. K-5	5 Titles
Foundations for Writing	Gr. 2-8	2 Titles
Home Study Collection™	Gr. 1-6	18 Titles
Literature Guides	Gr. 7-12	17 Titles
The Little Red Writing Books	Gr. 1-6	3 Titles
Math Whiz Kids™	Gr. 3-5	4 Titles
Novel Extenders	Gr. 1-6	7 Titles
On the Chalkboard™ for Reading & Writing	Gr. 1-6	6 Titles
Once Upon A Time™ for Emerging Readers	Gr. K-2	10 Titles
The Picture Book Companion	Gr. K-3	3 Titles
Quick Thinking™	Gr. K-12	2 Titles
Springboards for Reading	Gr. 3-6 & 7-12	2 Titles
Structures for Reading, Writing, Thinking	Gr. 4-9	4 Titles
Test Preparation Guides	Gr. 2-12	41 Titles
Thematic Units	Gr. K-8	23 Titles
Wake Up, Brain!!™	Gr. 1-6	6 Titles
Writing Warm-Ups™	Gr. K-6 & 7-12	4 Titles

To order, or for a complete catalog, write:

ECS Learning Systems, Inc.
P.O. Box 791439
San Antonio, Texas 78279-1439
Web site: www.educyberstor.com
or contact your local school supply store.

ISBN 1-57022-047-6

Table of Contents

Introduction

Teacher to Teacher: I was never taught to write. I was never taught how to teach children to write. My children struggled and I struggled while I tried endless "cute ideas." I never knew exactly what to say to the children. I read theories about writing. Typically, after reading a book of theories, I closed the book and said, "That's nice. Now what do I do?"

Finally, out of sheer desperation, I took what I knew about teaching and how children learn, and applied it to writing. This book is the result. It fills the gap between the theories and the children.

What is the best way to teach children to write? Read to children. Be excited about the books you read. Point out how an author develops the setting, the characters, and the plot. Discuss interesting words and interesting parts of the books. Encourage students to investigate and question an author's writing style. Create an environment that allows children to evaluate good literature. Your reading instruction is the vital support to your writing instruction. However, children do not learn to write simply by reading. And they do not learn to write by simply writing.

How do children learn to write? Some gifted students have a natural ability to read and to write. With little instruction, they see patterns and contextual clues in books and apply those concepts to their writing. However, the large majority of children need patterns to be pointed out to them. Even though children are not expected to "know" how to read, students are often expected to "know" how to write. Well-meaning teachers provide excellent models and exciting prewriting experiences. They then say, "Now you do it. Write about what you know." If a child happens to create a good composition, it is more likely to be by accident than from an understanding of what to do. If a child is unable to create a decent composition, neither the teacher nor the child knows what to do about it.

It seems a gross injustice to ask students to write without teaching them how to do it. The skills of crafting a composition, for most students, will not develop unless they are taught in the same manner that is used to teach reading, mathematics, or other subjects.

Most teachers have not been trained to teach children how to write. While there are volumes of books to help teach writing, most are either theories or isolated writing exercises. Teachers recognize good writing, but many are uncertain about how to teach it.

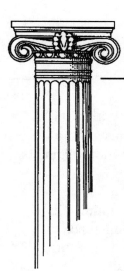

What can I expect from this book? This is the second book in a series. The first is designed for grades K, 1, and 2, and covers descriptions, stories, and directions. This book covers those topics, and moves on to compare/contrast (classificatory) and persuasive writing.

Writing has been singled out as a "different" subject. It is frequently taught simply by providing experiences in writing. Perhaps the fear is that suggesting guidelines will stifle creativity. The exact opposite is true. When children are uneasy about how to write, they are unable to concentrate on creativity in what to write.

Not all students will be best-selling authors. But all students can be taught to be competent writers. Bookstores are lined with references on how to write for publication. None of those authors are afraid to give directions on how to write to adults. Students deserve classrooms where they can learn the same structured information on writing skills.

Award-winning children's author Marion Dane Bauer in *What's Your Story?* says, "It may sound as if stories written by the formula…would be too much alike to be interesting. But that isn't the case. There is room for great variety within this simple structure. The formula exists, in fact, because storytellers have always tended to use it…And they have used it because it works."

The lessons in this book tell the teacher what to say about the patterns of good writing so that students learn to write. A connection between reading and writing is evident with quality literature selections serving as examples of writing skills to be learned.

This book teaches children to communicate. It does not address mechanics such as capital letters, punctuation, and spelling. If thoughts are organized and well developed, mechanics rarely impede the communication of ideas. However, the skills of mechanics should be modeled in the lessons and included as an integral part of editing in the writing process.

What about preparing students for writing tests? Many states are moving to testing programs which require students to exhibit a degree of mastery in written composition. This book is designed to train students to respond to testing formats, and has been proven to be highly successful for this purpose. Notes throughout the book give specific hints for testing situations.

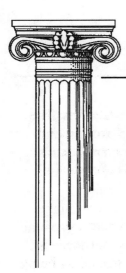

Some experts object to teaching children how to pass a test of writing skills. However, it seems wrong to ignore the reality that many students will be evaluated on written compositions. Students can be taught to write well and be prepared for testing at the same time.

The value of this book in preparing students for tests does not diminish its value in writing. Most "real life" writing experiences require adherence to directions, and the skills learned in this program are invaluable in guiding students through the expectations they encounter on a daily basis.

What about the writing process? This book encompasses the writing process. Students develop topics, write drafts, participate in conferences, revise, edit, publish, and share their work. This book tells teachers how to teach those parts of the writing process.

How do I integrate writing into my curriculum? Thematic units establish connections that support learning and long-term understanding. However, because many teachers are unaware of how to teach writing skills, thematic units often suffer in the area of writing. Writing is included, but it often consists of activities such as the following:

> Write a new ending to the story.
> Pretend you are a character in the story. What would you do?
> Tell about a time you had a similar thing happen to you.

These open-ended activities are fine, but only if the students have also been taught to write. Asking students to write is different from teaching students to write. Teachers need to be confident that they are teaching what students need to know about writing.

A better approach is to use the sequence of lessons in this book and connect the lessons to the thematic unit. Adapt the thematic unit to the writing lessons rather than the other way around. The literature references and the writing prompts in this book are suggestions. Other examples can be substituted by the teacher to connect the lessons to thematic units.

What about journal writing? Journal writing plays a vital role in the writing classroom. Young minds use journals to sort and develop ideas, respond to literature, come to conclusions about issues, and pull from the heart those thoughts that linger without expression until the journal opens the way. Journals can be particularly powerful, if not therapeutic, in helping students deal with the pressures of daily life that sometimes overshadow their ability to concentrate on "school stuff."

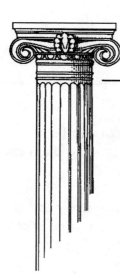

But asking students to write in journals is not teaching them to write compositions. Some journal entries may well be the nucleus of a piece of writing, but only if the student has been taught how to put the thoughts into a recognizable framework of communication. Again, asking students to write is not teaching students to write.

How do I use this book? The lessons are sequential and based on an ever-expanding foundation of competencies. Some lessons might be combined, but the order should be kept in sequence so that students are not frustrated by being asked to do something they have not been taught. Students learn that both literature and writing have a recognizable sequence.

The first ten lessons teach classroom procedures and routines rather than content. These procedures spell success for the writing program. Develop an atmosphere of trust, confidence, and acceptance regardless of the quality of writing during these lessons. Later, beginning in lesson eleven, students learn the content of writing.

When should I teach writing? Teach writing at the beginning of the day, or at the beginning of the class period. Teachers often begin class with what they consider to be critical subjects to "catch the students while they are fresh." Writing is a critical subject.

Scheduling writing at the beginning of the day or class has several advantages. Sometimes students are taught the strategy, "Do the hard parts first." That same strategy applies to teachers as well.

Another advantage of teaching writing at the beginning of class is the message of importance sent to students. Students learn that writing is a priority.

A third reason for teaching writing when class begins relates to the typical school day. "I was going to do _____, but we ran out of time" is a common teacher lament. If the writing curriculum is placed at the beginning of the class, it will not be skipped because time ran out.

How much time should I allow for writing? Set aside 20 to 40 minutes per day for writing. Many lessons in this book are designed for a single day. Other individual lessons provide directions to complete an entire composition, so a week of 30-minute writing sessions might be allowed for that lesson. Directions with each lesson give suggestions on how much time to allow for the various activities.

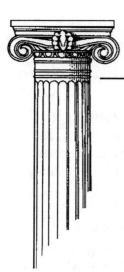

Skill lessons for older students may be 30 to 40 minutes in length. As they write independent compositions, full periods of 45 to 70 minutes allow them to develop ideas and reflect on their work in depth.

Where do I find that kind of time? Even if 30 minutes were magically added to the day, many teachers would still not teach writing because they would not know what to teach. This manual helps with that problem by providing the background of competence and the daily lesson plans for writing.

Still, time is rarely added to the school day. The only way to add instruction in writing is to drop instruction in another area. To simplify the problem by suggesting "integration" of writing with other subjects does not truly deal with the critical problem of lack of time. Even in an integrated curriculum, writing skills still require time for instruction that has not been allotted in the past.

The issue is not "How do I find time for writing?" but "How do I deny my students the right to learn a basic skill of literacy?"

Everyone finds time for priorities. While the final decision on what to delete lies with the individual teacher, the following suggestions may be helpful. The only requirements are an open mind to change.

1. Many teachers could benefit from "cleaning class" much like one might clean the garage. Look at the curriculum for items that could be eliminated. Are there some outdated lessons that no longer meet current needs? Are some activities kept because they are fun and have always been done? Are there some skills that could be taught as they apply to revision and editing in the writing process?

2. Evaluate the daily schedule, paying particular attention to transitional activities. Squeeze five minutes from one place and five minutes from another place. Cut transitional time to a minimum. Place an assignment on the board or transparency for students as they enter class.

3. Drop much of the spelling curriculum. Concentrate spelling instruction on high frequency words and letter patterns. Studies show that students learn to spell through reading and writing.

4. For some teachers, more time may not be needed. Use the lessons in this book as the writing program to assure that students are learning necessary skills to develop their abilities to communicate effectively.

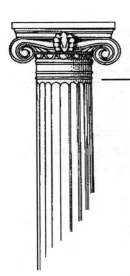

How fast should I proceed? The following schedule is suggested for a 36-week school year. If students are preparing for a competency test, set up a schedule that assures completion of the lessons before the testing date arrives.

Week	Lessons	Week	Lessons
1	1, 2	17	42
2	2, 3	18	43
3	4, 5, 6, 7	19	43
4	8, 9, 10	20	44, 45, 46, 47
5	11, 12, 13, 14	21	48, 49
6	15, 16, 17, 18	22	50, 51, 52
7	19, 20	23	53, 54, 55, 56
8	21	24	57
9	22, 23, 24, 25	25	58, 59
10	26, 27	26	60
11	28, 29	27	60
12	29	28	61, 62, 63, 64
13	30, 31, 32, 33	29	65, 66, 67
14	34, 35, 36, 37	30	68
15	38, 39, 40	31-36	A variety of prompts for practice
16	41		

An index of lesson objectives appears on pages 136-137 of the Appendix.

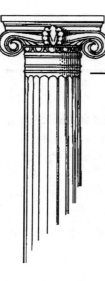

Management

☐ Stock the classroom with as many books as possible. Pay particular attention to the books listed at the beginning of the lessons. Request a set of books for your classroom from the school librarian. Rotate the collection with a new set of books every few weeks.

☐ Store writing supplies so they are readily accessible. Have plenty of pencils and paper available. Standard wide-ruled notebook paper works fine.

☐ Dedicate a large bulletin board to writing. This book includes numerous references to bulletin board displays that highlight the writing concepts being taught. The displays can be left up for the entire year.

Plan space for young authors to share their compositions with classmates. See page 128 of the Appendix for ways students can share their compositions.

☐ Give each student access to a thesaurus. The ideal classroom would have a student thesaurus for each student or pair of students. Perhaps a set could be checked out from the library, borrowed from other classrooms as needed, or brought from students' homes.

☐ Develop a large collection of pictures to supplement thematic units. A picture collection provides a gold mine of ideas for writing. Sources include magazines, catalogs, calendars, and posters.

☐ Provide each student with a portfolio folder for long-term storage of writing projects. It can be either a pocket folder or a standard manila folder. These folders are best kept as a class set in several boxes easily accessible to the students. One box is far too difficult for an entire class to use.

☐ Provide a daily pocketed folder for each student. This folder needs to include pockets and is kept by the student along with other textbooks. In each student's folder place the following:

1. A student booklet, Writer Reference, which will be used throughout the year. See page 140 for contents of this 20-page booklet. Bind or staple the booklet securely. Or, insert this booklet in the brads of the pocketed folder.

2. A half-sheet of lined paper stapled to the inside of the folder titled "Topics for Writing."

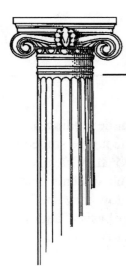

☐ When planning time for writing, keep in mind that some writing lessons can be completed quickly during a single writing period. Other, more extensive projects may span several days.

Students need to become accustomed to a writing routine developed early in the year. Part of that routine includes the idea that the writing period has a definite end. The writing project may not be complete, but the writing time has ended. This routine is important for several reasons.

First, students need to be comfortable knowing that writing is a process that takes time, often more than one day, and often more than two or three days. Completion is not the goal of a single writing period.

Second, students need to understand the value of stopping work on a project and coming back to it later. As a project is revisited the following day, students often see the missing words or the missing logic in what they wrote the previous day. This revision process is a standard practice among adults, and students need to learn the same process.

Third, when teachers adhere to the schedule they have developed for writing instruction, they will not resent the intrusion that writing has on their other subjects. It is fine, and necessary, to end the writing period so that other subjects can be taught.

When a writing period is over, instruct the students to store their assignments in their daily folders. Some students will exhale sighs of relief while others will groan in frustration because they are "right in the middle." Both reactions are acceptable.

☐ Erasers usually wear out long before pencils. Young students in particular want to please, and mistakes disrupt their work as they busily erase what they consider to be unacceptable. Erasing wastes precious time and derails the flow of ideas.

As students compose, encourage them to quickly cross out mistakes and continue writing rather than erase. Tell students you are interested in what their writing says, not how it looks on paper. Assure them that it is okay to be "messy." Explain that some of their compositions can be rewritten neatly or typed for display or sharing with other classes.

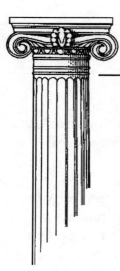

☐ The importance of spelling will vary from student to student depending on their own priorities and experiences with previous teachers. Encourage students to spell words as well as they can and to continue writing even if they have misspelled words. Invented or transitional spellings are fine. Tell students that the important part of their work is what words they select, not how they spell the words. Keep reminding students of this priority on a regular basis. Caution students never to stop writing while they wait for spelling assistance.

Do not expect students to write first drafts of compositions with a dictionary in hand. Nor is an alphabetical booklet of common words needed during a first draft. The laborious task of locating words in a dictionary, or even a booklet, impedes the thought processes required for putting ideas on paper. Attention to spelling is best left to the editing process.

As students work on a writing assignment, help individual students with spelling as needed. Ask students to open their Writer Reference booklet to the last page which is titled "Words for My Writing." When a student needs a word spelled, write the word on this page for the student to copy in the composition.

Another method of help with spelling is the development of a word bank at the beginning of a writing assignment. This activity not only provides students with needed spellings, but it also stimulates ideas for some students. The words can be copied in their Writer Reference booklets.

 ©ECS Learning Systems, Inc., San Antonio, TX

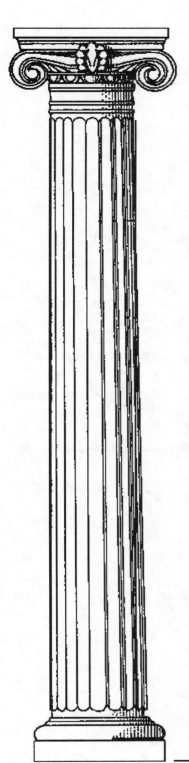

Descriptions

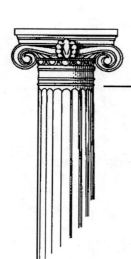

1

Objective

Students will develop topics for composition writing.

Materials

Daily writing folder for each student (see "Management," page 10)

Focus

Allow students to decorate or personalize writing folders as they wish. Explain that the folders will be a permanent part of their school materials, much like a textbook.

1. Instruct students to find the page "Topics for Writing" in their folders.

2. Using a brainstorming technique, generate a list of writing topics. Students should copy the ideas on the page "Topics for Writing." For example:

   my family
   my friends
   my house, my room, my kitchen, etc.
   my cat, dog, fish, hamster, horse, etc.
   what I look like
   my favorite food, animal, TV show, movie, song, subject in school, etc.
   vacation highlights
   my hobbies, collections
   lessons or special abilities
   life in _____ grade (current or previous grade in school)
   what I want to be when I grow up
   if I had a day I could do anything, I would...

Close

Comment positively about the lists of topics the students have developed. Explain that these lists will be used later only after you have taught them exactly how to write. Assure them that you will explain to them exactly what to do. Keep the classroom atmosphere positive and encouraging as the students begin their writing program.

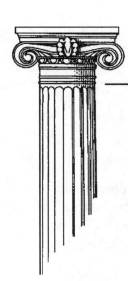

2

Objective

The students will learn writing routines in a whole-class composition.

Materials

Wide-ruled notebook paper or other paper to be used for composition writing; copies of students' compositions saved from previous years, if available; chart paper or blank overhead projector transparency

Note: This lesson teaches the following routines:

- Where to find paper
- Where to write on the page
- Brainstorming for topics
- Crossing out rather than erasing

Focus

Display and read some compositions from previous years. Explain that writing will be an exciting experience. Reassure students that they will never be asked to write something until they have been taught what to do. Tell students that for this first composition, the class will decide what to write.

Note: Some students' attitudes about writing may be negative. Others will be willing to try whatever is asked. Be particularly sensitive and reassuring to those who seem hesitant.

1. Ask students to date the top of their papers, which will be a daily routine. Later, these dates will help students see their progress as writers.

2. Using a brainstorming technique, ask students to name items or ideas related to school. Write the ideas on a chart or overhead projector. Examples might be: students, building, teacher, desks, cafeteria, library, playground, books, reading, math, chalkboard, paper, pencils, scissors, glue, tables, chairs, pictures, boys, girls.

3. Help students craft several sentences using information from the listed ideas. Write the sentences on the chalkboard or transparency, pointing out the capital letters, periods, and other conventions used in the sentences.

Note: Development of the composition depends on the age and skill of the students. Do not expect long compositions at this early stage. The objective for this lesson is to develop routines for writing. An example of a composition for young students for this lesson might be:

> This is Public School 112, located in Des Moines, Iowa. There are 25 students in our class, thirteen girls and twelve boys. Our classroom has student desks, a teacher's desk, and one long table. Many textbooks are on the shelves. Posters and rules are on the walls. We will learn about reading, math, science, social studies, and writing this year in school.

Note: Save the day's composition on chart paper or on a transparency.

4. Tell students to place an "X" at the beginning of alternate lines on their papers. Then instruct them to skip the lines marked with an "X" as they write. Encourage this routine until skipping lines for rough drafts becomes routine. Demonstrate on paper how to write the composition, skipping lines. Explain that the extra lines will allow for changes in their writing as they change their minds about what to write.

5. Instruct students to copy the composition on their papers. Remind students to skip lines and to refrain from erasing. Reassure them that it is fine to make mistakes, but the easiest way to correct mistakes is to cross them out and continue writing. Circulate among the students, encouraging them to skip lines and refrain from erasing. Both of these skills will require some practice.

6. Instruct students to place their completed writing in their daily writing folders.

Note: Students who finish quickly can be directed to further topics such as those listed on their "Topics for Writing" page. Discourage drawing pictures to illustrate the composition, so the students won't rush through the writing activity to get to the pictures. Art is a valid communication tool, but the emphasis needs to remain on written communication during the writing lesson.

Close

Remind students to skip lines and refrain from erasing as they write compositions.

Note: Do not ask students to recopy the composition neatly. If students feel that daily compositions must be recopied, they will learn to write as little as possible.

Note: This lesson may be repeated for several days, depending on the skills and needs of the students. The goal is to develop writing routines and self-confidence rather than accomplished pieces of writing. See Appendix, page 129 for further writing topic ideas for this activity.

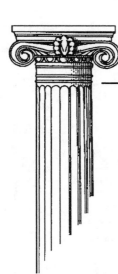

3

Objective

Students will revise and edit written work as a natural part of the writing process.

Note: This lesson may be repeated several days as needed.

Materials

Daily class writing from the previous lesson on a chart or transparency, a first draft of a composition written by an adult. If an original draft is not available, quickly write a brief composition, such as a friendly letter, and make some revisions. Content and competence are not important. The main idea is for students to see that adults revise and edit just as students do.

Focus

Show students the first draft of a composition. Let them see that when adults write, they, too, make changes. "Revise" means to make content and organizational changes. "Edit" refers to grammar and mechanics issues of punctuation, capitalization, and spelling. Explain that writing is different from other subjects in school. Writing is never correct the first time it is written. Therefore, they can remember not to be discouraged if their writing needs to be improved, because writers learn that revising and editing are important parts of writing.

1. Display a daily class composition from a previous lesson. Instruct students to reread it. Ask students for ways to change or improve the composition.

2. As changes are suggested, demonstrate how the skipped lines allow the changes to be made easily. Use cross-outs, the caret (^) mark, and other editing marks as needed to illustrate the editing and revision processes.

3. Instruct students to copy the new composition on their papers. Remind students to incorporate the corrections as they rewrite.

Close

All writers change their minds as they write. Review the importance of skipping lines as an easy way to allow for changes.

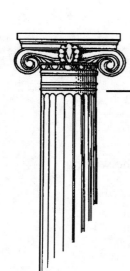

Objective

Students will learn to correct spelling errors.

Materials

Writer Reference booklet for each student (see "Management," page 10); class composition from previous lesson

Focus

Display class composition from previous lesson. Remind students that changes can be made after a composition is written. This is called editing and revising. Editing is a part of all writing. Skipping lines allows space for editing changes. Errors are crossed out rather than erased.

1. Instruct students to handle spelling problems by sounding out words and spelling words as well as they can. Remind students that you will not "count off" for spelling, and that you are more interested in what they write rather than in the spelling. Caution students never to stop writing because they do not know how to spell some words. Spelling can be corrected during the editing process. Worry about spelling can greatly inhibit creative thought processes as students write.

2. Tell students to circle words they are not sure how to spell and then continue writing until the editing process or until the teacher is available to assist. The circled words can then be checked and corrected when the teacher is available to assist and during the editing process.

3. Present each student with the Writer Reference booklet. Ask students to turn to the last page titled "Words for My Writing." Explain that this Writer Reference page can be used all year for help with spelling. Remind students to ask for spelling help by having Writer Reference and a pencil available. This routine will save frustration for both the teacher and the students.

4. Direct students to ask for spelling help only when the teacher is not busy with another student. Students should rely on their own ideas about spelling and should not stop writing while they wait for help from the teacher.

Note: Refrain from asking students to help each other with spelling. Later daily lessons provide many specific instructions for cooperative groups and interaction with classmates, but spelling help becomes disruptive. Students who are constantly asked for help with spelling have a difficult time writing their own compositions.

Close

Remind students that the routine for spelling has three parts:

1. Spell words as well as you can. Circle words you do not know how to spell. Never stop writing to ask for help with spelling.
2. Check to see if the teacher is busy before requesting help.
3. Have the last page of Writer Reference and a pencil in hand when asking for help with spelling.

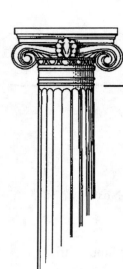

5

Objective

Students will create a composition using writing routines.

Materials

List of writing topics from lesson 2 or from Appendix, page 129

Focus

Review the writing routines students have learned:

- Skip lines.
- Cross out mistakes rather than erase them.
- Use editing techniques to make changes.
- Use the last page of Writer Reference to receive spelling help.

1. Refer students to writing topics listed in lesson 2 or Appendix, page 129. Also, investigate the literature students are currently reading for topic ideas.

2. Instruct students to select a topic independently and develop a composition using the models from previous lessons. They may write the composition in the manner that seems best for them. Prolific writers can be encouraged to add more detail to their compositions than class examples from previous days have included.

3. After about ten minutes, ask students to reread their compositions silently and to make editing changes. Circulate among the students, and make some editing suggestions either verbally or by writing with a pencil on their papers. Ignore most errors, but make positive comments. Keep an encouraging attitude. Remind students that revision and editing are part of writing.

4. Ask several students to share their compositions with the class. Emphasize that the appearance of the paper on the first draft is not a concern.

5. Ask students to save this composition in a portfolio. Determine a specific location and procedure for storing items in the portfolio. Without directions on how to place portfolio folders in a filing system, valuable class time will be wasted and folders will be lost.

Use the following procedures if a routine is not already in place:

- Supply several file locations. Do not expect an entire class to store folders in one place.
- Do not require folders to be alphabetized because it is time consuming. If students have been assigned a number, the number might be used to organize filing.
- All papers stored in the portfolio should be headed with date and name.
- Be sure the name tab is facing you so it can be easily read.
- Use one hand to hold back other folders in the box while placing the folder in the front. This prevents a folder from being placed inside someone else's folder.
- To add papers, remove the folder from the box, add the papers, and then return the folder to the box. Never drop papers in the folder without first removing the folder from the box because papers can slide into someone else's folder.
- Wait patiently while others finish using the box.

Close

Explain that portfolios will allow students to see their own progress in writing, and past compositions may inspire new thoughts for writing in the future.

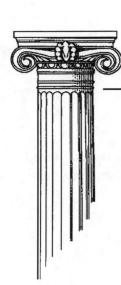

6

Objective

Students will participate in a prewriting activity.

Materials

The book *Woodsong* by Gary Paulsen or another book in which the author describes a passion for a particular activity; a small paper sack such as a lunch sack for each child; an item placed in one sack that relates to a favorite activity of the teacher (For example, a ski cap could represent a skiing hobby or a favorite book could represent a love of reading.)

Focus

Display the book *Woodsong*. Set the stage for listening by telling the students that this author has a way of writing that makes you feel like you are in the story.

1. Read passages from the book that explain the passion the author feels for dogs and dogsledding, particularly from chapter 7.

2. Ask students to think of an activity that they enjoy doing. Suggest that they think of their hobbies or their free time activities. Ask what they would do if they had twenty-four hours to do anything they chose.

3. Tell students they will be writing a composition about their favorite activity.

4. Give each student a small paper sack. Ask students to label the sacks with their names. As homework, instruct each student to put an item in the sack that depicts, symbolizes, or somehow relates to a favorite activity. Suggestions might be a favorite book, a photograph, a part of a collection, a piece of equipment needed for an activity, etc. Discourage students from bringing large, expensive, breakable items.

5. Share the item in the sack representing the teacher's hobby or free time activity. Explain its significance and importance, and that it is an example of the items the students might select for their sacks.

Close

Remind students to bring their item from home concealed in the sack for the next lesson and keep it a secret until their compositions are shared.

Note: This lesson and the following four lessons fully engage the students in the writing process. Even though students have not yet been taught how to write, this composition allows students to practice writing routines. The composition will be used later in the year for comparison to demonstrate progress in writing skills.

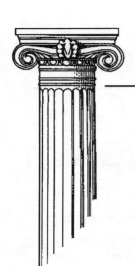

7

Objective

Students will begin writing a composition.

Materials

Special items each student brought from home; storage area for the student paper sacks; chart or transparency

Focus

Ask students to keep their special items concealed in sacks. Items will be shared at the end of the week when they display items and read their compositions to the class. Give specific instructions as to where the items are to be stored in the classroom during the week.

1. Tell students they will be writing compositions about their favorite activities. Quickly remind students of the writing routines they have learned. Explain that they will write, revise, edit, and rewrite in their best handwriting (or enter on a computer). This writing will be shared with the class and saved in their portfolios.

2. Using a brainstorming technique, list ideas that students might use in their compositions. Write the list on chart paper or transparency. For example:

   Describe the activity and special equipment needed for the activity.
   How often do you participate and how long you have been interested in it?
   How did you become interested in or how did you begin this activity?
   Why is this activity special to you?
   Describe a memorable incident you experienced while participating in or as a result of this activity.
   What do your family members think of your activity?
   Explain why other people might or might not enjoy this activity.
   Do you think it will always be special to you?
   Could this activity lead to jobs in the future?

3. Ask students to begin writing. Encourage them to use the suggestions above. Remind them to keep their objects hidden until they are shared at the end of the week.

Close

Instruct students to stop writing and place their materials in their daily writing folders. Explain that they will have an opportunity to work on the composition again.

©ECS Learning Systems, Inc., San Antonio, TX

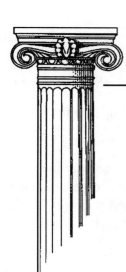

8

Objective

Students will continue a "work in progress," and begin revising and editing.

Materials

Special items from home; chart or transparency with the questions for stimulating ideas from previous lesson

Focus

Read the list of questions generated during the previous lesson. Instruct students to silently read their compositions which were started in the previous lesson.

1. Spend a few minutes in class discussion about the compositions. Ask students if they have particular problems or questions.

2. Instruct students to make revision and editing changes as needed, and then continue writing. Circulate among the students to check on their progress and their use of the writing routines established for skipping lines, crossing out, and obtaining spelling help.

3. Make positive suggestions to encourage writing, but do not make numerous corrections on the compositions. Ignore problems. Do not encourage the students to be dependent on teacher comments. These compositions are not expected to be accomplished pieces of writing, but will be used later for comparison to show progress. Maintain a positive, encouraging atmosphere and let students know they are performing well. It is extremely important to develop a positive attitude in students as they engage in writing. They must feel, "I can do it!"

4. Some students may announce, "I'm done!" When this happens, tell this student to reread his or her composition to see if there are revisions that could be made. If not, then direct the child to the page in the daily writing folder titled "Topics for Writing." Instruct the student to begin a new composition about one of the topics on the list.

   Handle this situation in a manner so that all students in the class understand what is happening. When students finish an assignment, they need to understand that there are two choices:

   • They may choose to make revisions in the composition using their editing skills.
   • They may begin a new composition while the rest of the students continue writing on the first assignment.

Some students will decide on the first alternative, investing more time in a single composition. This is to be encouraged.

Other students may have grown weary of a composition, and they would rather select the second alternative. Accept both decisions as valid. Over time, students rarely decide to write a second composition because they learn to express themselves so well in their writing. They prefer to fully develop one composition rather than write two short compositions.

The main idea is that the writing period is used for writing.

Close

Direct students to place their compositions in their daily writing folders. Remind them that during the next lesson they will need to finish this composition.

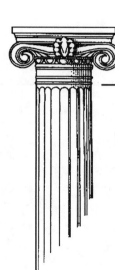

Objective

Students will rewrite a composition for publication.

Materials

A copy of the composition used in daily lesson 3 to illustrate how editing is an important part of the writing process; special items in sacks

Focus

Display the edited composition from lesson 3. Remind students that all compositions need to be read and revised so they can be improved.

1. Ask students to silently reread their compositions. They should look for revision and editing changes that can improve the writing. Do not insist on major changes since students have not yet been taught basic writing skills.

2. Instruct students to bring the composition to a close with one or two more sentences if it is not already ended. Even if students think they have more to write, insist that the compositions be ended quickly.

Note: Closure is a relief to some and a frustration to others. The prolific writer can be gently assured that the current composition will be fine if it is brought to an end as it stands. The ideas "still flowing" can be saved for later compositions. The prolific writer can sometimes be overwhelmed with a project if not encouraged to bring the composition to closure.

3. Explain that students are now ready to "publish" their writing. When a composition is published in a magazine or newspaper, it is typed and printed many times. In the classroom, publishing means that students write their compositions in their best handwriting or type them on a computer, making editing changes as they write.

4. Explain that this final copy needs to look nice, so careful erasing is permissible. This "publishing" activity can be assigned as homework.

Close

Instruct students to place their published compositions in their writing folders. Those students who are not finished can complete the work as homework.

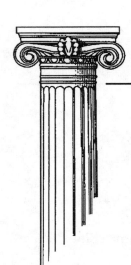

10

Objective

Students will share compositions with others.

Materials

Special items in paper sacks

Focus

Tell students that this is an exciting day because they will be sharing their writing and pulling their special items from the sacks to show the class.

1. Ask each author to read his or her composition to the class. As soon as a small group of students has completed their compositions, those students can begin sharing their compositions with each other, while others continue to finish their writing. More than one day will probably be needed for the sharing process, but it is essential that all students share their writing. If time becomes a serious issue, the class can be divided into two groups, with students reading their composition to half of the class.

2. Keep the atmosphere positive and encouraging. Praise each student's efforts.

3. Often, students are afraid to read their compositions, but they find that it is not difficult after they have tried it. Require all students to share their compositions. This is very important. Insist that even reluctant students share their work. If students are excused from the sharing process even once, it will be very difficult to persuade them to participate from then on. If one student is excused from the sharing process, the entire class learns this is permissible. Eventually, many students may decide they will not share their work.

   As each student reads his or her composition, the secret item from the sack can be displayed. Ask each student to explain the significance of the item to the activity described.

4. Model questions and positive feedback to the authors, and encourage the audience to participate with positive comments about the compositions. Examples might be:

   I like how you used the word _____ to describe your activity.
   You did a good job telling us how you spend time in your activity.
   You made me feel as though I would like to try your activity.
   Did you enjoy writing about your activity?
   What other objects could you have chosen to represent your activity?
   Are there some parts of your writing that you could change to make it better?

Close

Praise the students' writing efforts. Compositions may be displayed and later stored in the writing portfolios, or they may go directly into the portfolios.

Note: Sharing compositions is a critical part of the writing process. Never skip it. Sharing papers with classmates provides essential motivation for student writing. Knowing that an audience awaits their work, students strive to entertain and impress their peers. Sharing work validates the importance of writing. If work is not shared, students learn that the teacher is the only one who reads their work. They need to know that writing is communication with many other people, not just the teacher.

When students know that their writing will be shared with their peers, they tend to write with more care and enthusiasm, looking forward to the time when others will hear their work.

See the Appendix, page 128 for further suggestions on sharing written work.

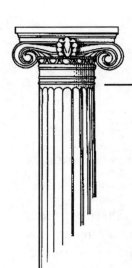

11

Objective

Students will recognize similes in descriptive writing.

Materials

Writer Reference; *As: A Surfeit of Similes* by Norman Juster; *Quick as a Cricket* by Audrey Wood; literature selections currently in use in the classroom or some of the following books:

> All *Harry Potter* books by J.K. Rowling
> *Pearl's Pirates* by Frank Asch, pages 27, 43
> *A Wrinkle in Time* by Madeleine L'Engle, pages 96, 97
> *My Side of the Mountain* by Jean Craighead George, pages 137, 139
> *I Am the Cheese* by Robert Cormier, page 1

Focus

Read *As: A Surfeit of Similes* or *Quick as a Cricket* to the students. Point out that the book is enjoyable partly because of the way the author uses words that make listening fun. Read some similes from the selected literature. Explain that similes help readers make pictures in their minds. Tell students that they will learn to write similes so that their writing will be interesting to read.

1. Reread a few similes. As you read, point out the similes used by the authors to create a clear picture of what they wanted to say. Similes are a creative and interesting way to show how two objects are alike.

2. Write the word "simile" on the chalkboard or transparency. Define simile as a comparison between two objects using the words *like* or *as*.

3. Write the word "fluffy" on the chalkboard or transparency. Ask students to think of something that is fluffy, such as a pillow, a bunny, a cloud, cotton candy, etc. Write *fluffy as cotton candy* on the chalkboard and explain that this is a simile. Write a complete sentence with the simile, such as *The packing material is as fluffy as cotton candy.*

Note: Students' similes are typically fresh and creative. Encourage their unique comparisons.

4. Ask students if they know other similes. Generate a quick list of similes the students may already know.

5. Direct students to turn to page 3 of Writer Reference. Quickly review these common similes to check for understanding.

©ECS Learning Systems, Inc., San Antonio, TX

Note: It is important for students to be somewhat familiar with common similes so they will understand meanings. However, common similes can be trite and overused. Encourage students to create their own similes, which tend to be far more fresh, vivid, and creative. Even one simile in a composition can add a great deal of interest and sophistication to the work.

Close

Review the definition of simile. Tell students that similes are fun to read and fun to write.

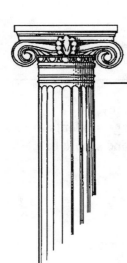

12

Objective

Students will create similes.

Materials

Writer Reference; rubber band, pencil, paper clip, other small classroom objects so that each small group or pair of students has one

Focus

Quickly review similes on page 3 of Writer Reference.

1. Ask students to create new similes using the ideas on the page. Write some of the interesting similes on the chalkboard. For example:

   The lamb is as white as popcorn.
   The computer screen is as smooth as laminated paper.
   The rug looks like brown tree bark.

2. Divide students into small groups or pairs. Give each group one item, such as a rubber band, a pencil, or a paper clip. Tell groups to write as many similes as they can about that item. Encourage students to write both kinds of similes, some using *like* and some using *as*.

3. After a few minutes, ask groups to share their creations. As similes are shared, write some of them on the chalkboard or transparency.

4. Challenge students to find similes as they read literature. Begin a collection of similes that can be displayed on a bulletin board or kept in a file or a class book for occasional reference and review.

Close

Praise students for their creative similes. Review the definition of simile, and explain that similes can add a great deal of interest to writing. Writing similes with both *like* and *as* could be a homework assignment.

13

Objective

Students will learn the importance of using interesting words in their writing.

Materials

Literature currently used in the classroom may be a good source of interesting word use, or passages from the following books:

> All *Harry Potter* books by J.K. Rowling
> *Fables* by Arnold Lobel (convenient because of interesting, short stories)
> *A Dog Called Kitty* by Bill Wallace
> *The Adventures of Huckleberry Finn* by Mark Twain
> *The Sign of the Beaver* by Elizabeth George Speare
> *Johnny Tremain* by Esther Forbes
> *Many Luscious Lollipops* by Ruth Heller
> *Knots in My Yo-Yo String* by Jerry Spinelli

Several newspaper accounts of sporting events. Select headlines that illustrate the different ways that newspaper writers say the same thing: one team won and another team lost.

A thesaurus for each student or small group of students (see "Management," page 10)

Focus

Remind students of the similes that they have learned to create and that similes make writing interesting to readers. Explain that they will begin learning another way to make their writing fun to read.

1. Read a passage from one of the literature selections. Ask students to listen for interesting words. Stop and discuss words as appropriate. Read some of the sentences again, substituting ordinary words to demonstrate how much better the story is the way the author composed it.

2. Explain that some words are very common and end up being "boring" when used repeatedly in writing. Good writers want to make readers interested in their stories, so they try to select interesting words.

3. Display newspaper accounts of sporting events. Read the headlines, pointing out how each one is saying the same message in a different way. People who read the sports pages would get bored reading "Someone won, someone lost" in each headline. Interesting words make reading more fun.

4. Give each student or group a thesaurus. Tell students that by using this book, writers find interesting words to include in their writing. Good writers, including adults, often use a thesaurus to add variety to their writing.

Note: If students are not familiar with a thesaurus, allow time to browse through the book. Note differences and similarities to a dictionary, and explain how a thesaurus is used.

5. Ask students to find pages 4 and 5 of Writer Reference. Explain that these pages will be used as a reference for writing along with a thesaurus.

6. Write the word "said" on the chalkboard. Ask students to locate this word in the thesaurus.

7. Point out that "said" will not be found in a thesaurus because it is a verb in the past tense. Ask students to think of the present tense of "said" (say), and find that word in the thesaurus. Remind students that the thesaurus will only include words in the present tense. As they are writing, they should locate the present tense of a past tense word they want to change.

Close

Review the importance of using a variety of words as a way to maintain reader interest. Ask students to bring newspaper headlines from the sports section or other examples of rich language from literature or media to class for the next lesson.

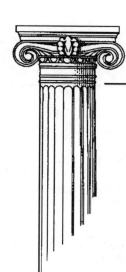

14

Objective

Students will develop a word bank as a reference for writing.

Materials

Newspaper accounts of sporting events from previous lesson or new examples from student assignments; a thesaurus for each student or group; Writer Reference

Focus

Read newspaper accounts and student assignments. Discuss the enjoyment that creative writing brings to readers because repetitive words are eliminated.

1. Ask students to work in small groups or pairs to complete the word bank on pages 4 and 5 of Writer Reference. It is not necessary for individual students to look up each word. Group sharing of synonyms is fine, since it saves time and yet serves the purpose of learning the treasures of a thesaurus.

2. Allow students to select any words on pages 4 or 5 of Writer Reference they would like to locate in the thesaurus. It is not necessary to fill in the blanks in any particular order.

3. If there are more than three synonyms listed in the thesaurus, tell students to select three they would like to include in their own books.

Note: It is important for students to spend some time completing the word bank pages of Writer Reference. They learn to be adept in the use of a thesaurus, and they are exposed to the variety of words available for use. The exercise sparks their creativity and desire for interesting words.

Note: Students may need extra time for this assignment, or it could be assigned as homework. It is not necessary for all lines to be completed in the word bank before moving to the next lesson.

Close

Point out that most of their favorite authors probably use a thesaurus as they write.

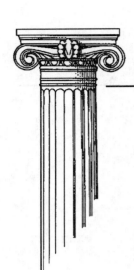

15

Objective

Students will learn how interesting verbs can improve sentences.

Materials

A thesaurus for each student or group; newspaper headlines about sporting events; literature passages using particularly interesting verbs such as:

All *Harry Potter* books by J.K. Rowling
The Hobbit by J.R.R. Tolkien
I Am the Cheese by Robert Cormier
Roll of Thunder, Hear My Cry by Mildred D. Taylor
Hank the Cowdog by John Erickson
Number the Stars by Lois Lowry
Ella Enchanted by Gail Carson Levine

Focus

Read the newspaper headlines and passages from the books.

1. Point out that often the powerful words in a headline or in a book are the verbs. Write some of the headlines and sentences from the passages on the chalkboard and underline the verbs.

2. Explain that interesting verbs that tell an exact action are perhaps the best way to create a visual image in the mind of the reader.

3. Write the following sentences on the chalkboard or transparency and underline each verb:
   He <u>started</u> the motor and <u>drove</u> away from the gas tank. Drover <u>came</u> out of nowhere and <u>got</u> up into the back of the pickup.

4. Explain to the students that these sentences are from *Hank the Cowdog*. In the book, the author John Erickson chose more powerful verbs than the underlined words. Ask students to suggest more interesting verbs to substitute for the underlined words.

5. Compare the students' suggestions to the words the author chose:

   He gunned the motor and pulled away from the gas tank. Drover suddenly appeared out of nowhere and hopped up into the back of the pickup.

6. Tell students that many verbs can be changed from ordinary, boring words to exciting verbs that create a vivid picture for the reader.

7. Follow the same procedure for these sentences from *I Am the Cheese* by Robert Cormier:

He <u>ran</u> out of the library, his books <u>held</u> in his arms, taking a moment to <u>look</u> through the window as Amy Hertz <u>went</u> to the circulation desk to <u>take</u> back her books.

Actual text: *He literally spun out of the library, his books clutched in his arms, taking a moment to watch through the window as Amy Hertz proceeded to the circulation desk to return her books.*

The man <u>put</u> a huge chunk of butter into the chowder and <u>smiled</u> at me.

Actual text: *The man dropped a huge chunk of butter into the chowder and grimaced at me.*

8. Ask students to work in pairs or small groups and follow the same procedure of improving the sentences below with vivid verbs:

She went to the cafeteria and got her lunch tray.
Winter is coming, and we want jackets.
The game was tied, and Mary sat on the bench.
The horse ran across the field with its tail in the air.
The mouse ran into a hole with a crumb in its mouth.
After a while, he went home and ate supper.

Encourage students to use a thesaurus and to be as creative as possible as they improve the sentences.

For example, the first sentence could be rewritten as follows:

She trudged to the cafeteria and retrieved a tray.

9. Ask groups to share their new sentences with the class. Write some of their new sentences on chart paper or a transparency for use in the following lesson.

Close

Remind students that interesting verbs greatly improve the quality of sentences. A thesaurus is a good source for interesting verbs.

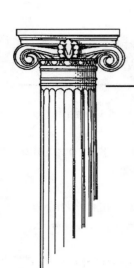

16

Objective

Students will improve writing with the addition of sensory adjectives.

Materials

Box of crackers; Writer Reference; bulletin board display of the five senses; literature used in classroom or one or more of the following books:

All *Harry Potter* books by J.K. Rowling
Knots on a Counting Rope by Bill Martin, Jr., and John Archambault
Across Five Aprils by Irene Hunt, pages 53, 175
The Haymeadow by Gary Paulsen, pages 32, 33
The Giver by Lois Lowry, pages 29, 175

Focus

Read passages from one or more of the books listed above. Show how the authors use the five senses to create images. Students can refer to the five senses to create meaningful descriptions.

1. Refer to the bulletin board display of the five senses. Remind students that our senses allow us to learn about our world. Using references to the five senses in writing helps readers better understand what is being communicated.

2. Give each student a cracker. Brainstorm a list of adjectives for the cracker. As each adjective is suggested, students should categorize it according to the sense it represents and write it under the correct heading on page 6 of Writer Reference. For example, the adjective "bumpy" would be listed under touch. Explore one sense at a time. Of course, the last sense will be taste, at which time the students eat the cracker.

3. As sight is discussed, encourage students to think of adjectives relating to shape and size rather than colors. Occasionally students become zealous about colors and ignore other comparisons. Color words quickly become trite.

4. Direct students to page 6 of Writer Reference. Because the words in Writer Reference are grouped in categories, this page becomes a valuable resource during writing along with the word banks and thesaurus. The list can jog memories and stimulate ideas for writing. Read and discuss words on the list as appropriate.

Close

Remind students that strong sensory details help readers make mental images and bring the composition to life.

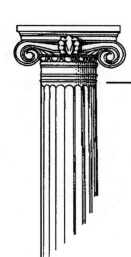

17

Objective

The students will write sensory adjectives correctly.

Materials

Literature selections from previous lesson; Writer Reference; a food item for class such as popcorn, dry cereal, wrapped candy, chocolate chips, marshmallows, peanuts, etc.

Focus

Read some descriptive passages from the literature selections. Remind students that the senses let the reader join the writer in the composition.

1. Direct students to Writer Reference, page 6, where adjectives for the cracker were listed in the previous lesson.

2. Ask students to compose a sentence about the crackers using at least some of the adjectives. Write a few of their suggestions on the chalkboard or transparency. For example:

   The cracker is square. The cracker is crumbly. The cracker is salty.

3. Illustrate how several adjectives can be listed in a sentence, and separated by commas, to make a more interesting sentence. For example:

   The square, salty cracker is crumbly.

4. Also illustrate how some of the adjectives might be transformed into interesting verbs. For example:

   The delicious, square cracker crumbled in my mouth.

5. Ask students to write several of the newly created sentences in the remaining space on page 6 of Writer Reference. These are examples of how adjectives can be rearranged to make an interesting sentence.

6. With a new food item, follow the same procedure. Brainstorm for adjectives and then arrange them into interesting sentences.

Close

Reread the simple sentences about the cracker and compare them to the newly created sentences. Remind students that sensory details in interesting sentences make the reader want to continue reading. As homework, students could write sensory details in interesting sentences about various food objects or items related to current literature.

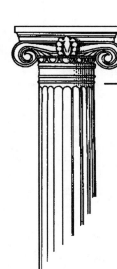

18

Objective

Students will create interesting sentences using sensory details.

Materials

A different food item (popcorn, dry cereal, wrapped candy, chocolate chips, marshmallows, peanuts, etc.) for small groups of students

Focus

Remind students of the previous lesson. Sensory details were combined to create interesting sentences. Today students will write sentences of their own.

1. Divide students into small groups or pairs, and give each group a different food item.

2. Direct students to list sensory words and categorize them according to the five senses.

3. Then have students write as many interesting sentences with sensory details as they can. Remind them to combine adjectives in a sentence by separating them with a comma. Remind them to look for ways to include interesting verbs.

4. Ask each group to share their sentences with the class. Comment on the creativity of each suggestion as it is made.

Close

On the chalkboard, write some very simple sentences about the food item. Compare it to the sentences that the students created. Remind students that they can now include interesting sentences like this in their own writing.

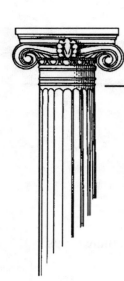

19

Objective

Students will expand sentences and rearrange information to create vivid writing.

Materials

Students' sentences from previous lesson; chart paper or transparency; bulletin board display of the following questions written on alarm clocks (to "wake up" writing): When? Where? Why? How?

Focus

Reread sentences the students wrote in previous lesson. Point out how word choice and also word position in sentences can greatly improve writing.

1. In addition to interesting word use, students can improve or "wake up" sentences by providing more information, or by expanding. Refer to the bulletin board display. To expand or "wake up" a sentence, add words or phrases to the sentence which answer at least some of the questions: When? Where? Why? How?

2. Write the following sentence on the chalkboard or transparency:

   The cat ran.

3. Ask students to expand or "wake up" the sentence by telling *when* the cat ran. Example:

   The cat ran yesterday.

4. Ask students to expand or "wake up" the sentence by telling *where* the cat ran. Example:

   The can ran to the barn yesterday.

5. Ask students to expand the sentence by telling *why* the cat ran. Example:

   The cat ran to the barn yesterday because it was hungry and wanted a mouse.

6. Ask students to expand the sentence by telling *how* the cat ran. Example:

   The cat ran quickly to the barn yesterday because it was hungry and wanted a mouse.

©ECS Learning Systems, Inc., San Antonio, TX

7. Ask students to improve the sentence by including interesting words and sensory details. Example:

    The scrawny, gray cat raced quickly to the rickety, weathered barn yesterday because it was famished and wanted a plump, juicy mouse.

8. This sentence can be improved further by rearranging the information to vary the simple subject-predicate form. Show the students how to place information into a subordinating phrase. Write the new sentences on chart paper or a transparency. Example:

    Yesterday, the cat, scrawny and gray, raced quickly to the rickety, weathered barn because it was famished and wanted a plump, juicy mouse.

    Or: Because it was famished, the scrawny, gray cat raced quickly to the rickety, weathered barn looking for a plump, juicy mouse.

    Or: In order to catch a plump, juicy mouse, the famished gray cat raced quickly to the rickety, weathered barn.

9. Compare the resulting sentence to the original idea: The cat ran. Answering the "wake up" questions *where? when? why?* and *how?* can greatly improve the quality of writing. Save these sentences for the following lesson.

10. Explain that the following words are often helpful in arranging sentence information into subordinating phrases. Refer to these words as "star writer" words because they contribute to "star writing." Ask students to copy these words on page 7 of Writer Reference as a resource for later writing:

after	before	though	whenever	while
although	even though	unless	where	as
as long as	in order that	until	wherever	if
as though	in order to	when	which	since
because	so that			

11. Explain that the basic procedure for improving sentences is:

    * Add sensory details.
    * Expand by answering the questions *where? when? why? how?*
    * Rearrange the information into subordinating phrases with "star writer" words.

Close

Compare the simple sentence with the expanded sentences to illustrate the improvement.

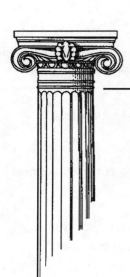

20

Objective

Students will expand and rearrange sentences by including information in subordinating phrases.

Materials

Writer Reference; sentences from previous lesson; literature currently used in the classroom or passages from the following books:

> All *Harry Potter* books by J.K. Rowling
> *Born Free* by Joy Adamson
> *Johnny Tremain* by Esther Forbes

Focus

Reread sentences created in previous lesson. Review the three-step procedure used to expand the original sentence:

- Add sensory details.
- Expand by answering alarm clock "wake up" questions.
- Rearrange information with "star writer" words.

1. Copy a sentence from the previous lesson or a literature selection on the chalkboard or a transparency. Place brackets around the first four words. Explain that if the subject and the predicate of the sentence are both in those first four words, the sentence can be often improved by rearranging information with "star writer" words. For example:

   [The cat ran to] the barn yesterday because it was hungry.

2. Show that by moving some information to the beginning of the sentence, the repetition of "subject-predicate" form can be avoided. For example:

   [Because the cat was] hungry, it ran to the barn yesterday.

3. Point out that the use of brackets around the first four words helps identify the need for rearranging a sentence.

Note: Not all sentences need to be rearranged. However, extensive practice of this skill needs to be provided so that students can avoid simple sentences when appropriate.

4. Ask small groups or pairs of students to expand and rearrange these sentences:

    The cup fell.
    The wind blew.
    The pig oinked.
    The water spilled.

5. Direct students to place brackets around the first four words of each sentence and check the placement of the subject and the predicate. Encourage students to make further revisions of the sentences.

6. Direct students to copy several of the expanded sentences on page 6 of Writer Reference and use them as reminders of the procedure used to expand sentences.

Note: Practice this skill until students feel confident. Any simple sentences can be presented for practice.

Close

Reread some sentences the students created. Comment on how "waking up" sentences with "star writer" words greatly improves writing.

Assignment for next lesson: Ask each student to bring a mystery item from home that will fit in a lunch sack. The item can be an ordinary household object, such as a washcloth, pencil, spoon, etc., or it can be an item of special interest such as a part of a collection, a piece of sporting equipment, etc. Ask students to keep the object a secret from classmates.

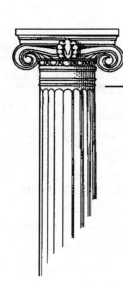

21

Objective

Students will write a composition integrating acquired writing skills.

Note: This lesson may last several days. The purpose is to incorporate similes, interesting words, and sensory details into expanded, complex sentences. Organization of compositions follows in later lessons and should not be the focus at this point.

Materials

Student items from home (assignment from previous lesson)

Focus

Review skills in similes, interesting words, sensory details, and expanded complex sentences.

1. *Prewrite:* Ask students not to show their objects to anyone. Instruct students to examine their objects for details and possible descriptive words.

2. *Write:* Tell students to begin a composition describing what is in their sacks, using writing skills learned thus far. Remind students to skip lines while writing. When they have finished, they will read the descriptions and ask the audience to guess what objects are inside.

3. *Edit/Revise:* Now that specific skills have been acquired, students can edit and revise their work by looking for certain qualities in the sentences. Put the following list on a chart or transparency, and ask students to use crayons or colored pencils to underline the items accordingly in their compositions:

   similes using *as* - green
   similes using *like* - yellow
   interesting words and sensory details - orange
   "star writer" words - place a small star by the words

   Tell students to add information if those items cannot be found.

   Ask students to place brackets around the first four words of each of their sentences. If the subject and predicate are found in the first four words, students should rearrange the sentences with subordinate phrases using "star writer" words.

©ECS Learning Systems, Inc., San Antonio, TX

4. *Publish/share:* Students should publish their descriptions by rewriting or publishing on a computer. The compositions can be read to classmates. The audience tries to guess what the objects might be.

   Compositions can be bound in a class book titled *What Am I?* After reading each description, the correct answer for each item can be written on the back of each page. Students can illustrate the objects for the book. Send home copies of the book for parents to read with the students. A book like this can also be shared with another class or a younger grade level.

Close

Point out the qualities of good writing the students displayed in their mystery bag descriptions. Mention their use of imaginative similes, interesting words, sensory details, and complex sentences. Writing that makes clear pictures in the minds of readers will be enjoyed and appreciated.

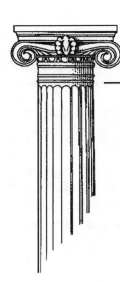

22

Objective

Students will learn ways to organize descriptive writing.

Materials

Transparency copies of child, alligator, and bird (Appendix, pages 130 and 131); bulletin board display of these phrases: "top to bottom," "side to side," "main focus"; literature related to current unit of study or passages from the following books:

> *My Side of the Mountain* by Jean Craighead George
> *A Wrinkle in Time* by Madeleine L'Engle
> *The Sign of the Beaver* by Elizabeth George Speare
> *The Haymeadow* by Gary Paulsen
> *The Secret Garden* by Frances Hodgson Burnett

Focus

Read some descriptive passages from literature. Point out how the author uses description to help readers paint mental pictures and to feel as though they are eyewitnesses "at the scene" in the book.

1. Descriptions play an important role in many compositions. Skills in writing descriptions can be incorporated into compositions later.

2. Descriptions are best understood if they are organized in a logical sequence.

3. Refer to the bulletin board display of organizational strategies for descriptions. Most scenes, characters, and pictures can be organized in one of three ways:

    -   Top to bottom
    -   Side to side
    -   Main focus

4. Display the picture of the child. Discuss how it would help a reader if a writer described this picture from top to bottom. Point out how difficult it would be to understand a description if the author started with the hair, then shoes, then eyes, then belt, etc. To help the reader follow the ideas, the description can begin at the top and move down the body.

5. With a projection pen, number items in the picture in order from top to bottom. For example:

   1-hair, 2-face, 3-vest, 4-shirt, 5-pants, 6-shoes

   Discuss the importance of using a logical order rather than jumping from place to place.

6. Display the picture of the alligator. Discuss how it would help a reader if the writer described this picture from side to side. Most animal pictures lend themselves to the "side to side" organization, progressing from head to tail. With a projection pen, number the items in the picture in the order from side to side. For example:

   1-mouth, 2-teeth, 3-eye, 4-back or body, 5-legs, 6-tail

7. Display the picture of the bird. Many pictures and scenes have several items to describe. The writer should first select a main focus of the picture, describe it fully, and then move to the details around the main focus. With a projection pen, number the items in this picture in the order they could be described. For example:

   1-bird's head, 2-worm, 3-bird's body, 4-wing, 5-baby birds, 6-nest, 7-leaves/branch

8. Give each pair or small group of students two or three laminated pictures and an overhead projection pen. Students should determine the best organizational strategy for describing the pictures and number the pictures.

9. Ask groups to share their numbered pictures with the class as you discuss the strategies used for each picture.

Close

Refer to the bulletin board display to review the three organizational strategies for descriptions. Place a picture example beside each strategy.

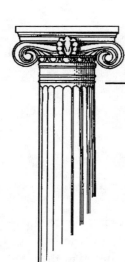

23

Objective

Students will develop a reference list of sequence words for use in writing.

Materials

Writer Reference

Focus

Write several sequence words such as *next, finally, first, after that* on the board or transparency. Explain that sequence words help readers know where their mental picture should focus. Even when a description is well organized, sequence words act like road signs to keep the reader on the right route.

1. Explain that sequence words can tell *order* and also *when* something happens.

2. Instruct students to find page 8 of Writer Reference. Ask them to list the sequence words from the board and brainstorm more words to complete the list. This will serve as a permanent reference for future writing. The list should include: then, just after, first, second, third, last, soon, meanwhile, now, finally, next, in conclusion, after.

3. Caution students to use each sequence word only once in a short composition. Sequence words are important, but they must not become repetitious. Extensive use of the ordinal numbers (first, second, third, fourth, fifth, sixth, etc.) also becomes repetitious.

4. Explain that sequence words can easily be inserted into a composition. Each numbered item in a description can be introduced with a sequence word. During the revision process, students can check for sequence words if they were omitted from the first draft.

Close

Sequence words show that writing is well organized. Remind students that sequence words can easily be added during revision.

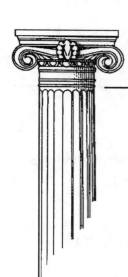

24

Objective

Students will include the location of items in a descriptive composition.

Materials

Writer Reference; inflated balloon or other interesting object; any large picture with many items in it; literature from current study or passages from the following books:

> *The Secret Garden* by Frances Hodgson Burnett, page 13
> *The Haymeadow* by Gary Paulsen, pages 110, 111

Focus

Read passages from literature that tell the location of items or characters. Explain that telling where an item is in a picture helps a reader make a clear mental image.

1. Use the balloon to demonstrate location words such as *over, under, beside*. Instruct students to find page 8 in Writer Reference. Using a brainstorming technique, generate a list of location words that could be used in writing. Students should write the words in Writer Reference for later use. Include such words as: over, under, underneath, next to, in back of, above, down, down from, at the base, touching, in front of, on top, outside, inside, to the right or left, on the edge, away from, alongside, around, surrounding, between, beyond, behind, across from, against, bordering, adjacent, adjoining, touching.

2. Show students a large picture. Ask students to suggest sentences describing the location of items in the picture.

Close

Review the importance of writing sentences that tell location as a way to make descriptions more meaningful for readers. Remind students that location words can be added easily during revision if they were omitted during the first draft.

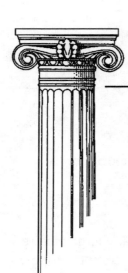

25

Objective

Students will expand a description by including actions, purposes, or feelings.

Materials

Transparency copies of girl, alligator, and bird (see Appendix, pages 130 and 131)

The Skin I'm In by Sharon G. Flake
The Little Prince by Antoine de Saint-Exupery

Focus

Explain that descriptions can be lifeless without some action, purpose, or personal feeling added to the description. Sentences can be included to give action, purpose, or feeling to each item in a picture.

1. Read the first chapter of *The Skin I'm In*. The character's reaction to the new teacher makes the description come alive.

2. Read the first several pages of *The Little Prince*. Point out how the little boy's feelings about his artwork and his actions give readers an important dimension of understanding and an association with the pictures.

3. Display the picture of the girl. Ask students, as a class, to create a sentence about the girl's hair. Remind students to include location words, interesting verbs, similes, and sensory adjectives when possible. For example:

    On each side of the little girl's head, ribbons swept her blond hair into pony tails.

4. Ask students to create a new sentence telling some action, or a purpose, or a personal feeling about the hair. For example, one of the following would be acceptable:

    Action sentence: The ponytails bounced in the breeze like cheering pom poms.
    Purpose sentence: The ribbons prevented her curly blond hair from falling in her face.
    Feeling sentence: The pony tails seemed to turn her into a jumping jack.

5. Move to other items in the picture and repeat the procedure as a class. Write two or three sentences about each part of the picture until students seem to grasp the concept. Examples for the vest might be:

> Action sentence: The vest wrapped her in dazzling colors.
> Purpose sentence: The vest completed her "first day of school" outfit.
> Feeling sentence: The bright alphabet letters dancing on her vest let you know she was ready for school.

6. Continue this procedure with other items in the picture and with other pictures until students feel some confidence with the activity. Point out that only one of the sentences is needed for a description, but practice the three different types so they understand what is expected.

7. Select another picture and, as a class, practice writing three sentences about an item in the picture:

   - The first sentence should give a description of the location.
   - The second should describe sensory details written in a complex style, perhaps including a simile.
   - The third sentence should convey some action, purpose, or feeling regarding the object.

Close

Discuss the merits of the students' writing. Remind students that descriptions come alive when action, purpose, or feeling is added to the composition.

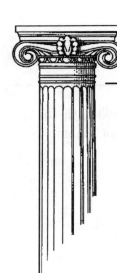

26

Objective

Students will apply writing skills to a class descriptive composition.

Materials

A picture on a large poster or, preferably, copies of the picture for each student; transparencies

Focus

Quickly review the bulletin board display of writing skills which have accumulated from previous lessons. Explain students will now apply those skills to a composition that is written as a class.

1. Explain that the class will write a description as a cooperative effort. Many ideas will be needed, but not every idea will be used.

2. Display the picture prompt. Ask students to determine the best strategy to organize the picture. Number the picture accordingly, including as many numbers as reasonable.

3. Elicit three or more sentences about each numbered item. The first sentence should include a description of the location. The next sentences should include sensory details written in a complex style, and perhaps a simile. The last sentence should convey some action, purpose, or feeling regarding the object.

4. Write student responses on the transparencies. Allow space on the transparency for later revisions. Allow students to see how ideas should be recorded quickly during this first draft.

5. As you record the sentences, demonstrate how to indent the first sentence of a paragraph. Begin a new paragraph for each new item that is described.

Note: Move quickly through this class writing exercise. Encourage all students to participate, but keep the flow of the writing moving rather than insist that all students make a contribution. Quiet students can listen and learn from classmates as the composition develops.

Allow students to suggest ideas, but do not be afraid to suggest your own ideas if they seem appropriate. The purpose is to provide a model of writing.

Do not insist on perfection. Spend 30 to 45 minutes writing. Keep the writing moving quickly so the students see the complete "beginning-to-end" process. The first draft stresses creativity and organization rather than perfection.

Save the transparency composition for the next lesson.

Close

Reread the composition to the students. In the next lesson, students will revise and edit the composition.

Note: Class compositions, as described in this lesson, should be written routinely before each independent writing assignment so that students know what they are expected to do. The emphasis is on content rather than appearance.

Class compositions serve three purposes:

1. The composition is a model of what students are expected to do. The students see a composition develop from beginning to end.

2. Students see how to revise and edit a first draft.

3. Involvement with the writing process as a class spurs independent creative thinking.

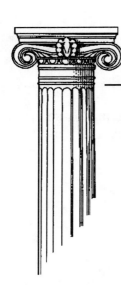

27

Objective

Students will revise with the aid of writing checklists and color codes.

Materials

Transparency copy of the composition from the previous lesson; duplicated copies of the writing checklist (See Appendix, page 132. Have many copies available in a place accessible to the students.); a "color" editing chart for bulletin board display; projection pens to match colors of display. Students also need crayons or colored pencils to correspond to the display:

similes using *as* - green
location words - red
star words - draw a star
sensory details - purple

similes using *like* - yellow
interesting words - orange
sequence words - blue

Focus

Display copies of the checklist. Explain that the list will be a guide for writing and editing descriptions, and will be used by the teacher for evaluation. The checklist can be modified to meet the needs of the students.

1. Review the checklist items with the students. Instruct students to use the checklist as they write, revise, and edit. When items from the checklist are included in the compositions, students can check those items.

2. Refer to the color codes on the checklist. Explain that students should underline the designated items with the corresponding color. If some colors are missing from the composition, the missing items can be added.

3. Using the checklist as a guide, generate a class revision of the description from the previous lesson. Use colored projection pens to underline items which should be included in the composition. Ask students to revise by adding items from the checklist which are missing.

Close

Reread the revised composition and comment positively on the quality of writing. Remind students to use the checklist each time they write a description.

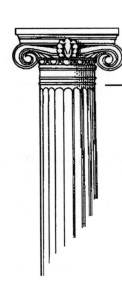

28

Objective

Students will apply writing skills to a descriptive prompt.

Materials

A collection of descriptive picture prompts (see "Management," page 10). Allow students some choice in the prompt. They will be more motivated about the assignment if allowed that choice. Children's books are excellent sources of pictures for descriptive writing. Caldecott winner books are particularly good choices.

Note: This lesson will span a period of days.

Focus

Review the process needed to write a descriptive composition:

- Decide on an organizational strategy.
- Number the picture according to that strategy. Encourage detail by determining at least eight or ten numbers.
- Write three or more expanded sentences about each numbered item. The first should include the location. The next sentences should include sensory details written in a complex style, and perhaps a simile. The last sentence should convey some action, purpose, or feeling regarding the object.
- Begin a new paragraph for each numbered item.
- Revise and edit using the checklist and color code. Place brackets around the first four words of each sentence to check for simple sentences.

1. Instruct students to write individual compositions and apply the skills they have acquired.

2. Students should revise and edit their work.

3. Students should publish their work in neat handwriting or on a computer.

4. Reward the students' effort. Share compositions with classmates and other audiences as available. See the Appendix, page 128 for suggestions.

Close

Praise the students' efforts in their writing. Ask students to file their compositions in their portfolios. They can compare this composition to the earlier composition and note progress in their skills.

Notes on classmates' comments: The following method of editing can be beneficial as students learn to listen to classmates' compositions for qualities of good writing.

When students read their compositions, give each student in the audience a card with a word printed on it. Words on the cards come from the checklist, and several cards can have the same word:

> sequence words, location words, interesting words, sensory details, simile, repetition, correct tense, star words, complex sentences

After the composition is read, the audience gives quick comments about the part of the composition listed on their cards. For example, if a student holds a "location" card, then that student reports on the inclusion of location words in the composition. Students exchange cards after each composition is read so they have different responsibilities.

This activity has several benefits. The audience has specific reasons for listening. Also, the comments are specific so that the author gets excellent feedback on the positive parts of the writing.

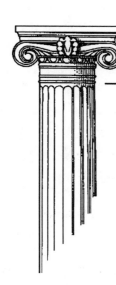

29

Objective

Putting it all together:

Allow students to write two descriptions independently before moving on to stories. At least one could be homework. After the first assignment, certain skills and issues will become evident as topics for reteaching. Dramatic improvement will be noted in their next compositions.

Provide a variety of prompts and allow the students to select the prompts, or encourage students to find their own prompts in books, posters, or photographs.

As each writing assignment is introduced, write a class composition to model expected outcomes.

Before each individual assignment, review the procedures to follow in writing. For most students, one revision of the first draft is the most they will be willing to manage. Do not strive for a perfect paper from each student. Writing skills develop with practice, guidance, and maturity. Each composition should show growth, but not necessarily perfection. Remind students that writing is never finished, and that improvement comes with learning skills and with practice.

At this point, students can be evaluated on their writing abilities. Do not write on the compositions, but rather let the checklist be the primary evaluation tool. Check or star each item on the checklist that is present in the composition. Make notes as appropriate on the checklist. Return the checklist to the student as a record of your evaluation or as a prescription for further revision. Date and save the checklist in the writing portfolio along with a copy of the composition. They serve as evidence of progress and as a record of weak areas that need reteaching or practice.

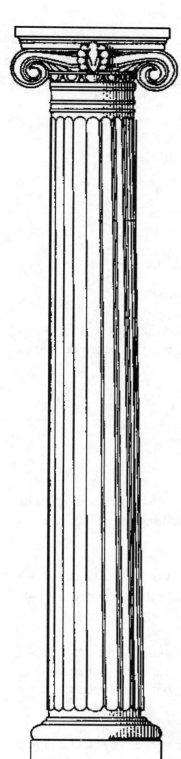

Stories

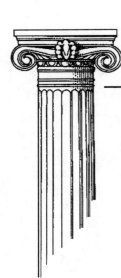

30

Objective

Students will learn the qualities of story prompts.

Materials

All *Harry Potter* books by J.K. Rowling
Hank the Cowdog by John Erickson
Woodsong by Gary Paulsen
The Secret Garden by Frances Hodgson Burnett

Or, examples from current classroom literature in which the action of the story is organized around particular sites; Writer Reference; bulletin board display of the following narrative writing prompts:

Tell about the adventures of...
What happened while (the character) visited (a place)...
Write a story about his (or her) day...

Focus

Review the meaning of "narrative" as telling a sequence of events. To narrate means to tell what happened, and this lesson begins a series of lessons on how to write one kind of narrative, a story.

1. Quickly review the action and settings from one or more books. Point out that description is a vital part of the books, but the action is the key to making the story come alive and become interesting.

2. Ask students to list the various sites used in one or more of the books. Write responses on the chalkboard. Point out how the author may have used the sites to organize the book. It is possible that the author determined several sites and then developed the story action around those sites.

3. Emphasize that there are many ways to organize a story, but authors always use a plan to structure their writing. One good plan is to select a series of sites, and then develop adventures which happen at the sites.

4. Refer to the bulletin board display to point out that this simple plan works particularly well for writing prompts containing the following key phrases:

Tell about the adventures of...
What happened while (the character) visited (a place)...
Write a story about his (or her) day...

Note: Following directions is a major criterion of success in most day to day activities for students and adults alike. To receive credit for writing on a standardized test, students must respond correctly to the writing prompt. For example, if the prompt asks for a description, the student must describe rather than write a story. If the prompt asks for a story, the student must write a story rather than simply describe. This distinction should be strongly emphasized and reviewed frequently in classrooms where students will be tested.

Close

Review the three story prompt phrases. Remind students of the importance of reading prompts carefully to determine the response they should make in their compositions.

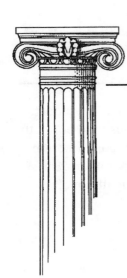

31

Objective

Students will learn the qualities of story introductions.

Materials

Sentence strip with the following phrase: "Once upon a time..."; bulletin board display with the following words: kind of day, times, sites, actions; transparency copy of page 133 in the Appendix, "Story Introductions"; some of the following literature:

Knots in My Yo-Yo String by Jerry Spinelli
I Am the Cheese by Robert Cormier
Ramona and Her Father by Beverly Cleary
Abel's Island by William Steig
The Story of Helen Keller by Lorena Hickok
The Best Present Ever by Jean Marzollo
The Thief by Megan Whalen Turner
My Side of the Mountain by Jean Craighead George
Dragon's Gate by Laurence Yep

Focus

Display the sentence strip "Once upon a time..." Ask students if they understand the phrase. Most will say it is the beginning of a story, but they will not be able to say much else about it. Often the phrase is used because a writer is unable to think of a better way to begin. Tell students that even though many good student stories begin with this phrase, better introductions are easy to write.

1. Emphasize the importance of introductions. Good introductions catch the interest of the reader and make the reader excited to read the rest of the story. A poor introduction may cause a reader to stop reading. Good introductions help set the stage and direction of the composition.

2. Read the introductions to one or more of the books listed above. Some introductions last two paragraphs. Read enough so that the four components of introductions are evident: kind of day, time, site, action.

3. Ask students to visualize the setting presented in the introductions. Because the authors have written interesting introductions, readers feel like they are "in" the story, and they want to hear more.

4. Refer to the bulletin board display of the four parts of an introduction. Explain that good introductions will include all four items within the first few sentences or paragraphs. Students will learn how to do each part in future lessons.

5. Using the "Story Introductions" transparency, categorize the components of one or more of the book introductions. For example:

Story Introductions

Book Title	Kind of Day	Time	Site	Action
I Am the Cheese	cold	ten o'clock October	Route 31, Monument, Massachusetts	riding a bicycle

6. Point out that not all good introductions contain all four parts, but most introductions will include at least some of the four parts.

7. Point out that the introductions to many books may last for several sentences or even several paragraphs, but that the basic components will be evident.

Close

Compare "Once upon a time..." to an introduction from one of the listed books. Ask students which one is more interesting. Review the importance of writing good introductions. Reread the four parts of a good introduction. Ask students to watch for good introductions in books they read.

Possible assignment: Using current classroom literature, ask students to categorize the introductions into the four components. Remind students that all four parts may not be present in every introduction.

Note: Many stories that begin with the phrase "Once upon a time..." go on to include the parts of good introductions. The phrase is used here for comparison purposes and to encourage students to be more creative and explicit in their introductions.

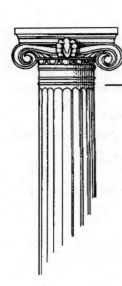

32

Objective

Students will include the kind of day in story introductions.

Materials

Weather report from local newspaper; chart paper or transparency with the following sentence: "One day I went to the park" (This sentence will be expanded in later lessons, so save space underneath the sentence for future, improved sentences.); Writer Reference; transparency copy of "Story Introductions" (page 133 of Appendix); literature from previous lesson, titles listed below, or other stories in which the kind of day is evident in the introduction:

A Wrinkle in Time by Madeleine L'Engle
Bridge to Terabithia by Katherine Paterson

Focus

Review student homework assignments as a class. Use the transparency "Story Introductions" to categorize the four components as students share homework.

1. Read the weather words from a newspaper weather report. Explain that telling about the weather, or kind of day, enhances introductions because it helps readers make clear pictures in their minds.

2. Using a brainstorming technique, generate a list of weather words which students should copy on page 9 of their Writer Reference books. Words to include: hot, cloudy, sunny, dark, windy, rainy, cool, freezing, warm, stormy, snowy, cold, balmy, breezy, drizzling.

3. Display the sentence "One day I went to the park." Ask students to improve this sentence with a reference to the kind of day. For example:

   One sunny day I went to the park.

   Write the new sentence under the original sentence and save for future lessons.

Close

Compare the original sentence to the new sentence created with the addition of the kind of day. The expanded description helps the reader form a clear picture.

©ECS Learning Systems, Inc., San Antonio, TX

33

Objective

Students will include time and sites in story introductions.

Materials

Introductory sentence from previous lesson; Writer Reference; literature from previous lessons or current thematic literature from classroom

Focus

Read the introductions from one or more of the books. Discuss how the author used time and sites in the story to help the reader understand what to expect.

1. Using a brainstorming technique, generate a list of time words which the students should copy on page 9 of Writer Reference. For example: spring, summer, fall, winter, last year, last month, names of months, names of days, names of holidays, last week, yesterday, last night, many years ago, on my last birthday, when I was a baby, early morning, mid-day, late afternoon, after school, dawn, dusk, twilight, midnight.

2. Display the introductory sentence "One sunny day I went to the park." Ask students to improve the sentence with a reference to time. For example:

   One sunny day last summer I went to the park.

   Write the new sentence under the previous sentence.

3. Using a brainstorming technique, generate a list of sites which the students should copy on page 10 of Writer Reference. Encourage students to list sites they have visited because these will help develop their best stories. For example: pond, river, riverbank, their room, swimming pool, beach, mountains, mall, circus, ocean, airport, train station, football stadium, soccer field, movie theater, farm, ice skating rink, museum, playground, library, front porch, kitchen.

   The list of sites is nearly endless. Stores are also good sites. Examples include: grocery store, toy store, shoe store, sporting goods store, ice cream shop, restaurants, book store, bank, gas station, video store, etc. Calling a store by its particular name is fine, but don't encourage students to list names of stores in Writer Reference because the list may end up including only names of stores. Tell students to expand the lists to include as many different kinds of sites as possible.

Note: Some younger students limit story sites to common choices such as park, woods, zoo, and space. These sites are not only common, but they are difficult to expand because most students have not spent much time in the woods or in space, for example. Sometimes forbidding students to use these common sites forces them to be more creative in their writing.

4. Display the previous sentence: One sunny day last summer I went to the park. Ask students to suggest a more interesting site to improve the introduction. Write the new sentence under the original sentence. For example:

    One sunny day last summer I went to a garage sale.

Close

Compare the original sentence to the improved introduction. Point out that adding the time and site to the introduction helps the reader know what to expect.

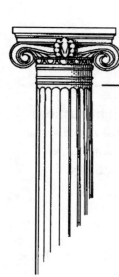

34

Objective

Students will write interesting actions in story introductions.

Materials

Literature from previous lessons; Writer Reference; thesaurus; examples of narrative writing prompts. Prompts can be pictures or statements such as:

Pretend you were "teacher for a day" (or substitute any profession). Tell about your adventures for the day.
Tell about your trip to...
Tell about a day with a friend.

Focus

Read the introduction from one or more of the books. Point out the interesting action that happens in the introduction. Introductions can be boring if the only activity is "went." Explain that actions usually relate to chosen sites, and therefore it is difficult to generate a list of actions appropriate for the many possible sites. However, students can create a valuable list of synonyms for "went," an often overused verb. These words often fit nicely in introductions.

1. Using a brainstorming technique, generate a list of synonyms for "went," which students should copy on page 11 of Writer Reference. For example: jumped, glided, skipped, zoomed, ambled, strolled, pedaled, trotted, moseyed, sashayed, hopped, scooted, scurried, hurried, scrambled, hustled, stomped, marched, strutted.

2. Suggest that students use a thesaurus to generate more interesting actions.

3. Display the sentence from previous lessons. Ask students for an action that could make the introduction more interesting. For example:

   One sunny day last summer I pedaled my bicycle to a garage sale.

4. Remind students that good introductions may use several phrases, sentences, or paragraphs to tell about the four components of introductions. The lists developed for Writer Reference serve as catalysts in writing those passages.

5. Display several writing prompts for a narrative composition. Explain that the introductions must make sense with the prompt. A prompt that refers to a train ride would not make sense with swimming. In addition, the action must make sense with a site from the prompt. A prompt that refers to school would not make sense with a mountain climbing activity.

Close

Compare the original sentence to the new introduction. The new introduction, while fairly simplistic, is acceptable and far better than the original sentence.

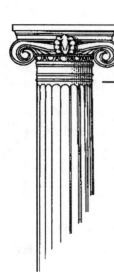

35

Objective

Students will create two styles of story introductions.

Materials

Writer Reference; bulletin board display of introduction styles: straightforward and quote; sample narrative writing prompts (a collection of pictures on any subject that can be used for practice introductions; pictures from current units make excellent prompts for introductions); transparency of "Story Introductions" from page 133 of Appendix; literature from previous lessons or:

Dragon's Gate by Laurence Yep
Cry, the Beloved Country by Alan Paton
Two of a Kind by Beatriz Doumerc and Ricardo Alcantara
Indian Captive by Lois Lenski
Skylark by Patricia MacLachlan
The Great Gilly Hopkins by Katherine Paterson

Note: While introductions should not be written in isolation, they can be practiced and improved as they are in this lesson without completing an entire composition. As students develop confidence in writing good introductions, the confidence carries on through the writing process.

Focus

Read some introductions from literature, pointing out the style of the introduction: straightforward or quote.

1. Explain that the four components of introductions can be included in the first several sentences or paragraphs in different ways. One of the two basic styles is a straightforward sentence that begins to identify the parts of the introduction. This is the most common type of introduction, and a very effective one. Often the straightforward sentence contains an element of shock or mystery to jolt the reader's attention.

2. A second introductory style is to quote a major character. This style is particularly effective because it immediately puts readers "in" the story as they imagine the character talking. The quote can be a statement or a question.

3. Display the prompts. Ask students individually or in small groups to select a prompt and write a story introduction, involving a major character from the prompt, that will make a reader want to keep reading. Remind students that introductions can be several sentences long so that appropriate detail and interest can be developed. The sentence writing techniques learned in previous lessons regarding similes, sensory details, interesting words, and complex sentences should be an integral part of the introduction.

4. Ask students to share their introductions with the class. As they are read, categorize the four components on the "Story Introductions" chart, and identify the style: straightforward or quote.

Close

Comment about the quality of the student introductions. Emphasize the importance of a good introduction as a way to catch the reader's interest. A carefully written introduction also allows the writer to confidently launch the writing assignment.

36

Objective

Students will organize a story.

Materials

Writer Reference; sample story prompts (or a collection of pictures that can serve as writing prompts); transparencies or chart paper; bulletin board display of story outline (shown in # 5 below); literature from classroom study, or the following:

> All *Harry Potter* books by J.K. Rowling
> *The Adventures of Ali Baba Bernstein* by Johanna Hurwitz
> *The Incredible Journey* by Sheila Burnford
> *Johnny Tremain* by Esther Forbes
> *Where the Wild Things Are* by Maurice Sendak
> *Three Days on a River in a Red Canoe* by Vera B. Williams

Focus

Remind students that a story must be organized so it will make sense to the reader. Point out that the organizational strategies for descriptive writing will not work for story writing.

1. The story action can be organized around sites. These are the same sites developed for use in introductions. For teaching purposes, students should be encouraged to select only three sites. Even older, advanced students should be encouraged to create a framework of only three sites, so that action can be fully developed at each site. Too many site changes will impede the flow of the story and cause the reader to feel like the story is jumping from place to place.

2. Display a prompt as a subject for a class composition, and ask students to suggest three sites for the story. Remind students that often the prompt will suggest a beginning site which should obviously be the first site on the list.

3. Before writing any story, students should select three sites and write those three sites at the top of the paper. Write the three sites at the top of a transparency or chart paper. Explain that these three sites will help them develop the rest of the story.

4. As a class, ask students to generate an introduction that involves a major character from the prompt in one of the two introductory styles. Write the introduction on the transparency or chart.

5. Display the story writing outline. Explain that this is the guide for development of a story, and the introduction is already finished. Ask students to copy the outline on page 12 of Writer Reference.

    Introduction
    Brief description
    First site - three events
    Transition
    Second site - three events
    Transition
    Third site - three events
    Conclusion

6. Use the outline to discuss the next writing step, which will be a brief description of the main character. After the introduction, readers want to become better acquainted with the main character before more action takes place.

7. Read the first several pages from *Harry Potter and the Prisoner of Azkaban*. Point out that the author set the stage in the introduction, and then allows the reader to become better acquainted with the main character.

8. Writing the brief description is quite simple because it requires the skills already learned in writing descriptions. All of the extensive detail practiced in writing descriptions does not need to be included. Students should select the most important, major characteristics to describe.

9. Briefly discuss the remaining items on the outline and explain that the composition will be developed in the following lesson.

Close

Review the story outline and the importance of selecting three sites before beginning the story.

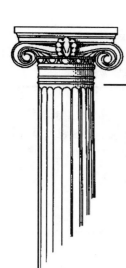

37

Objective

Students will write the body of a story.

Materials

Transparency or chart with introduction from previous lesson; Writer Reference

Focus

Review the organization of the story outline on page 12 of Writer Reference. Read the introduction from previous lesson.

1. Continue writing the composition as a class by composing a brief description of a major character. Write student responses on the chart or transparency.

2. To continue the story, refer to the beginning site. Because the introduction sets the stage for the beginning action and plot, continue to develop at least three or more actions that occur at the beginning site. As the class generates the composition, write the suggested sentences on the transparency or chart. Caution students to be aware of the following issues as they develop action at the sites:

    •   Avoid complicated problems to solve. Compositions with problems to be solved will be learned in future lessons. To prevent confusion and frustration at this point, encourage students to focus on a simple story of three events at each site without creating difficult, unmanageable problems.

    •   Avoid allowing a character to be hurt or lost. These events are common student choices, but are very difficult to handle successfully in a story. Encourage students to create more interesting actions.

    •   Whenever possible, develop actions around events students themselves have experienced. The best writers tell about what they know, and young writers should be encouraged to pull from their own experiences for writing inspiration.

3. Divide the class into small groups or pairs. Assign several groups to develop at least three events at one of the remaining sites, and several other groups to develop three events at the third site.

Close

Ask groups to share their events. As a class, select one group's story for each of the two remaining sites to be included in the whole class story.

 ©ECS Learning Systems, Inc., San Antonio, TX

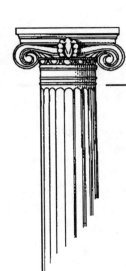

38

Objective

Students will write transition sentences in stories.

Materials

Transparency or chart copy of whole class story and group compositions from previous lesson

Focus

Reread the introduction, brief description, and action at the first site that were developed as a class in the previous lesson. Explain that this lesson will incorporate their group work into the composition with the use of transition sentences.

1. As a class, decide which of the remaining two sites should come next in the composition. The next task involves moving major character(s) from one site to the next with the use of transition sentences. Transition means a move from one place to another. Transitions allow the reader to move logically with the character from one site to another. Without transition sentences, the narration becomes illogical and abrupt.

2. To write a smooth transition, first visualize the first site and the action at that site. Determine a good reason for the character to leave that site and a way for the character to move to the next site. Ask students to generate a transition sentence or sentences that tell why and how the character changed sites. Write the sentence on the chart or transparency.

    Suggestions for *why* the character moved: got hungry, was exhausted, ran out of money, had an appointment, needed something at a store, needed to repair an item, played on an organized team in which the game was over, the movie or party was over, etc.

    Suggestions on *how* the character moved: rode bicycle, skipped, galloped, loped, zoomed, skated, flew, skateboarded, strolled, rode taxi (bus, train, subway, etc.)

Avoid simple transitions such as "The (character) decided to go to ____ and so she went." Avoid introducing new characters that tell the main character to go somewhere else.

3. In the same manner, generate a transition between the second and third sites and copy it on the transparency.

Close

Reread the entire story, making small editing changes as needed. Tell students that they will write the ending in the next lesson.

39

Objective

Students will write conclusions to stories.

Materials

Class composition from previous lesson; one of the following books:

Two of a Kind by Beatriz Doumerc and Ricardo Alcantara
Andy and the Lion by James Daugherty
Mooncake by Frank Asch
Not This Bear! by Bernie Myers
The Ghost-Eye Tree by Bill Martin, Jr. and John Archambault
Barn Dance! by Bill Martin, Jr. and John Archambault

Focus

Explain to students that a good conclusion is an important part of writing. Readers need to know that the story is over. A good closing lets the reader feel comfortable about putting the story away because it is clear that a stopping place has been reached.

1. "They lived happily ever after" is a typical, trite ending that often closes a story because some writers are not sure what else to say. Another common, trite ending says, "Then I went home." Endings can be abrupt and leave the reader jolted and unhappy if they are not written well.

2. Read one or more of the books listed above. Show how the ending relates to the beginning. While these books are literature for younger children, they are universally enjoyed by all ages, and they clearly illustrate a straightforward technique to writing story endings. Explain to older students that these books are much shorter to read to the class than an entire book used currently in the classroom.

3. A successful technique for writing endings relates to the story beginning, particularly in the short stories students are writing. Tell students that when they come to the end of their compositions, they should read the introduction again. The introduction provides ideas for what to say at the end. The conclusion should relate to the beginning in terms of time, place, and action. The activity that was happening in the beginning should be stopped in the ending. For example, if the major character was riding a bike in the beginning, then the conclusion should say that the bike ride is over.

   Caution students not to introduce a new character that announces an activity is over or that the major character needs to be somewhere else. Also caution students to avoid getting tired or going home at the end. These activities end up being trite and uninteresting.

4. A second part of the ending should tell how the character feels. For example:

   The (character) had a great adventure and couldn't wait to take that trip again.
   Or: The (character) had a great adventure and learned that libraries can lead to exciting times.

5. A third part of the ending can tell what the character plans for the future. For example:

   From now on, the (character) will be spending a lot of time at the library.

6. Using those three components (stop the beginning activity, tell character's feelings, and tell future plans), develop a conclusion to the class composition. The ending might take several sentences, but shouldn't be long and confusing.

7. Read the introduction to a children's book. Without reading the rest of the book, ask students to generate some logical endings to the book. Practice this skill as needed with the class.

Close

Reread the entire class composition. Review the procedures for writing endings:

1. Stop the beginning action.
2. Tell how the character feels.
3. Tell the character's plans for the future.
4. Don't introduce new characters.
5. Don't go home.
6. Don't get tired.

©ECS Learning Systems, Inc., San Antonio, TX

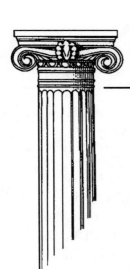

Objective

Students will revise and edit a story.

Materials

Class composition from previous lessons on chart paper or transparency; student copies of the narrative writing checklist from page 132 of the Appendix

Focus

Reread the class story from previous lessons. Point out how the composition developed according to the outline for story writing.

1. Distribute copies of the story checklist. Ask students to read the checklist and notice differences from the descriptive checklist. Many items are the same on both checklists. The checklist can be modified to meet the needs of the students.

2. Use the checklist as a guide to revising and editing the class composition. Use colored projection pens to underline the color-coded items from the checklist.

Close

Read the final version of the composition and compliment students on their creativity.

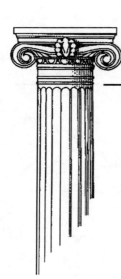

41

Objective

Putting it all together:

Depending on the age, writing experience, and needs of the students, this outline may be the only tool needed for story writing. A second story outline involving story problems is presented in lessons 42 and 43. The introduction, brief description, and conclusion remain the same, but the alternative outline provides a new and interesting perspective on story writing.

Give students the opportunity to write two compositions with this outline before proceeding to the next lessons. After the first independent writing assignment, areas for reteaching will be evident. Do not expect perfection. The second composition should show marked improvement.

Encourage students to select pictures as the catalyst for stories, or to develop their compositions from their own ideas.

For students preparing for a standardized test, the prompts should consistently reflect the format of the test. It is difficult to transfer writing skills to new formats without plenty of practice. They need to be very comfortable with the testing format to fully demonstrate their writing abilities.

As each writing assignment is introduced, compose a class story to model expected writing proficiencies and to stimulate ideas. Continually review the steps to follow in writing the story.

Begin each independent writing period with directions for students to read carefully what they have written the previous day before they continue.

Always provide opportunities for students to share each of their compositions. Never skip this important part of the writing process. Check page 128 of the Appendix for ways to vary the sharing process.

When you evaluate compositions, make notes on the checklists rather than on the compositions. Save and date the checklists and the compositions in the portfolios.

For most students, listing three sites for the composition provides ample preplanning. The ideas for activities usually develop naturally as they progress with their writing through the outline. Many accomplished authors begin with only the simplest of plans in mind.

However, some students seem to "ramble" or have unusual difficulty progressing with a story. Ask these students to develop a more complete outline before beginning to write. For example, ask students to list the three sites and also the three actions at each site before they begin to compose. Discourage the use of complete sentences, but rather emphasize that the list can later be developed into sentences for the composition. After this thorough outline, students are less likely to stray from the main ideas and forget the organizational strategy.

This complete outline technique should not be forced on all students. While it is helpful to some, it may become cumbersome and confusing to others. Rather, teach the complete outline to those students whose writing indicates a need for more structured preplanning.

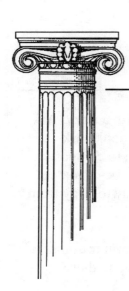

42

Objective

Students will learn a second organizational method for story writing.

Materials

Writer Reference; bulletin board display of narrative outline for story problems:

1. Introduction
2. Brief description of major character
3. Describe the problem. Include these sentences:
   "The problem was..."
   "The problem happened because..."
   Tell how the character felt.
4. Try to solve the problem. Include these sentences:
   "(Character) tried to solve the problem by..."
   "This idea didn't work because..."
5. Solve the problem. Include these sentences:
   "The problem was finally solved when (character) had a plan. The plan was..."
6. Closing

Note: This lesson should last several days. Allow for practice of the outline.

Focus

Point out that many entertaining narratives involve a major character who encounters a problem and solves it through the course of the composition. A different organizational strategy can be utilized for writing narratives which involve a problem to be solved.

1. Point out that the new organizational strategy has many basic components that remain the same: introduction, description of major character, and ending. All the skills of writing similes, sensory descriptions, and complex sentences are applied to the new strategy.

2. Refer to the bulletin board display to introduce the new outline. Direct students to copy the outline in Writer Reference, page 13.

3. Explain that the outline requires very specific sentences to be included. Those sentences are designed to keep the story moving toward a conclusion in a logical progression. Insist that the specific sentences be included in compositions to provide the necessary

organization. Some advanced writers may be able to write without the specific sentences listed in the outline. However, most students benefit greatly from the structure that the outline and the specific sentences provide.

4. Explain that each part of the composition needs to be full of details and action. To further expand a composition, part four can be repeated one or more times.

5. Some possible topics might include: bothersome siblings, schoolwork or grades, broken toys or possessions, being late, deciding what to wear, homework, substitute teacher, keeping bedroom clean, biting fingernails, computer problems, finishing chores, making decisions about where to go or what to do, or needing to earn money.

6. Tell students to avoid the following problems: fights, "getting mad" at someone, being lost, getting chased, or a character being hurt or killed. These problems are very difficult for young writers to bring to a satisfactory conclusion, and will dominate writing unless students are forced to consider other kinds of problems.

7. Encourage students to write compositions in which the major character does the problem solving. Avoid "quick fixes" such as "They called the police" or "Their mother came..." Avoid introducing new characters who show up to solve the problem. Keep story characters to a minimum, and allow them to solve the problems with their own initiative.

Close

Review the new outline, explaining that it can be an exciting alternative for narrative compositions. Using the outline assures that the composition progresses toward completion.

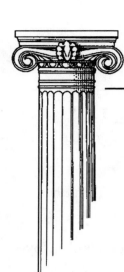

43

Objective

Students will practice writing a composition with a story problem.

Materials

Bulletin board display of story problem outline

Focus

Review the outline for story problem writing.

1. As a class, write a complete composition using the new outline. Keep the composition progressing quickly through the outline, to model how the students' creative ideas can be structured.

2. Use the story checklist to model the process for revising and editing.

3. Be sure students have the opportunity to share their compositions.

4. Assign two independent writing projects using the new outline before moving to the next lessons. Do not expect perfection. After the first assignment, areas for reteaching will be evident. Expect marked improvement on the second assignment.

5. Date and save all checklists and compositions in students' portfolios.

Close

Review the two outlines for story writing. Point out the differences and similarities. Most writing prompts will allow students to select which outline they want to use.

Again, allow students to write at least two compositions with this outline before moving to the next genre.

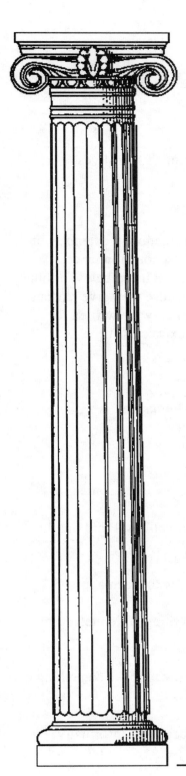

Directions

44

Objective

Students will learn the importance of informative writing in their lives.

Materials

Games such as Monopoly, Scrabble, Clue (including directions); examples of hobby and travel books/magazines; directions for a household appliance; a teaching manual for reading, math, or other subject; books listed below or other "how to" books. The first two are particularly good because they give reasons and details for each step of the directions. Even though they are written for younger children, they make the point without taking extra class time.

The Pottery Place by Gail Gibbons
Making Bread by Ruth Thomson
Action Contraptions by Mary and Dewey Blocksma
Fifty Nifty Origami Crafts by Andrea Urton

Focus

Display books, games, and directions. Explain that these materials tell how to do something.

1. Read some game directions, a book, and household appliance directions. Point out that each part of the directions is carefully explained.

2. Display a teaching manual. Read parts that give directions on how to teach a lesson.

3. Tell students that these materials are examples of informative writing which tell factual information. Directions are one kind of informative writing.

4. A writing prompt for directions will ask for an explanation of how to make something or how to perform a task.

5. Prepare students for the writing task by telling them that the process for informative writing will be simple:

   Make a detailed, chronological list of steps needed to accomplish the task.
   Elaborate the steps with details, reasons, and examples.
   Write an introduction and a conclusion.

Close

Review the importance of informative writing and the steps to accomplish the task.

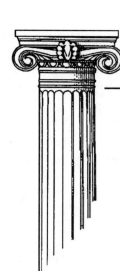

45

Objective

Students will participate in a prewriting activity for writing directions.

Materials

Chart paper or transparency; an activity for a prewriting experience, preferably one that most students would not have had experience with in the past. For example:

> how to do a particular science experiment
> how to use a piece of equipment such as a laminating machine or a book binder
> how to make a recipe such as pancakes or other food item

Focus

Explain that students will be participating in an activity that they will use later as the topic of their directions. Remind students to watch carefully for the chronology of each step, materials needed, and reasons for each step.

1. Allow students to participate in the prewriting activity. If another person is doing the demonstration, mention important points as the demonstration progresses. Name materials and parts; discuss reasons for each step.

2. After the demonstration, ask students to tell each step of the demonstration in the order that it happened. List the student responses on a transparency or chart paper. Encourage students to include as many detailed steps as they can remember.

3. If necessary, combine some of the steps so that six or seven steps become the basis of the composition.

Close

Tell students that making a chronological list of steps needed to accomplish a task is the first step to writing directions.

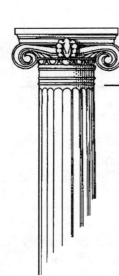

46

Objective

Students will elaborate directions with details, reasons, and examples.

Materials

The Pottery Place by Gail Gibbons or *Making Bread* by Ruth Thomson; chart paper or transparency; list of steps from previous lesson; bulletin board display:

Elaborate Directions
    Details - location and description
    Examples - compare to something else
    Reasons - tell importance or why that step is done

Note: Examples for this lesson are related to a prewriting activity in which the students learn to make pancakes.

Focus

Read one of the books. Point out how the author fully explained each step of the process. Examples and reasons for each step make the ideas clear to the reader.

1. Read the list of steps generated in the previous lesson. Reaffirm that the list is in correct order and includes all the steps necessary to accomplish the task.

2. Elicit student suggestions on writing the first step in sentence form. Write the sentence on the chart or transparency. For example:

   Assemble all needed materials.

3. Refer to the bulletin board display. Explain that details in directions include location and description which are writing skills acquired in previous lessons. Ask students to suggest some details to elaborate the first step.

   Most details can be incorporated into the original sentence. Encourage students to expand the sentence rather than write a separate sentence to add details. Write the suggestions on the chart or transparency. For example:

   Assemble a bowl, spoon, griddle, measuring spoons, measuring cups, and all needed ingredients.

4. Refer to the bulletin board display. Point out that examples are often comparisons to some other ideas or objects. Ask students to elaborate the first step by providing a comparison. Add the sentence to the chart or transparency. For example:

   This is like collecting all the pieces to a puzzle before putting it together.

5. Refer to the bulletin board display. Explain that directions make sense when reasons or explanations are provided for each step. The use of "star words" is one way to add reasons to directions. Ask students to provide reasons or explanations for the first step. Add the sentences to the chart or transparency. For example:

   By assembling all materials before beginning to cook, the pancakes can be made quickly and efficiently.

6. Assign the remaining steps of the demonstration to small groups of students. Instruct each group to write the step in sentence form, and elaborate with details, examples, and reasons so that each step has three or four sentences.

7. Assemble student group work in the correct order and read the entire composition to the class.

Close

Explain that writing directions is quite easy. After listing the steps to the process in chronological order, elaborate each step with details, examples, and reasons.

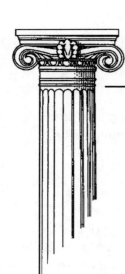

47

Objective

Students will write introductions and endings to directions.

Materials

Directions generated in previous lesson; transparency or chart paper; Writer Reference; bulletin board display of directions outline:

Introduction - state topic and importance
Tell each step - elaborate with details, examples, reasons
Conclusion - directions are complete, restate use

Focus

Reread the whole class composition written in the previous lesson.

1. Ask students to recall the beginning of the demonstration, pointing out that there was a statement about what they were going to learn and why it was important.

2. Explain that introductions to directions should include two parts. Ask students to compose statements including these two parts.

    A. A statement of the topic. For example: Pancakes are a popular breakfast treat.
    B. A statement telling the importance of or uses for the directions. For example: By following simple directions, even a beginner can turn out pancakes fit for a queen.

3. Conclusions for directions include two parts. Write an ending with these parts:

    A. A statement that directions are complete. For example: This completes the directions on how to make pancakes.
    B. A restatement of the use for the directions. For example: These directions can be used by anyone who wants to make their own pancakes from scratch.

4. Direct students to copy the directions outline in Writer Reference, page 14.

Close

Review the steps and the outline for writing directions.

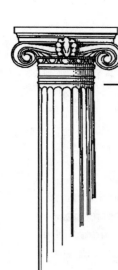

48

Objective

Students will revise and edit directions.

Materials

Composition generated in previous lessons; student copies of writing checklist for directions, page 134 of Appendix

Focus

Reread the directions generated in the previous lessons. Point out that the writing is clearly organized to allow the reader to understand what is being learned.

1. Revising and editing are important parts of writing directions. The directions must be very clear so that the reader can accomplish the task independently.

2. Use the writing checklist for directions to revise and edit the class composition. Pay particular attention to the importance of sequence words. Because directions usually require steps to be followed in a certain order, the use of sequence words is particularly helpful. The checklist can be modified to meet the needs of the students.

3. Remind students to indent each new step of the directions.

Close

Read the revised directions. Comment on the positive aspects of the composition and praise the students' efforts.

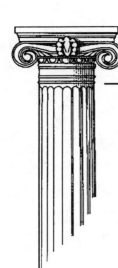

49

Objective

Putting it all together:

Provide students the opportunity to write two independent compositions on directions before proceeding to the next lessons. Do not expect perfection. After the first independent project, topics for reteaching will be evident. Students should show marked improvement on the second independent assignment. Always allow time for sharing the compositions.

Date and save compositions in students' portfolios.

Suggested topics need to be evaluated carefully to determine whether or not all students have the background experience to fully develop the directions.

One way to guarantee that students have the necessary background experience to write directions is to provide the experiences at school. Use hands-on activities from across the curriculum as topics for directions. Art projects, science experiments, demonstrations, cooking activities, social studies projects, and activities in physical education classes can be developed into directions. Look at the daily routine for topics that could be developed. Ask school personnel and community members to demonstrate a procedure used in their jobs.

Ask students to think about their activities at school and at home. Discuss interests and hobbies. Simple routines that are part of the lives of most students can be developed into directions. For example:

    care for an animal - washing, feeding, training
    develop and care for collections - rocks, stamps, baseball cards, dolls, etc.
    play a musical instrument
    play football, basketball, baseball, etc.
    make a lunch, a cake, cookies, main dish, salad, pizza, sundae, etc.
    wash hair, brush teeth
    set the table
    clean the kitchen, garage, room, etc.
    knit, cross stitch, crochet, sew, etc.
    wash the car
    mow the lawn
    care for/ride a bike
    swim, water ski, snow ski, roller skate, ice skate, roller blade
    go fishing
    give a party

    ©ECS Learning Systems, Inc., San Antonio, TX

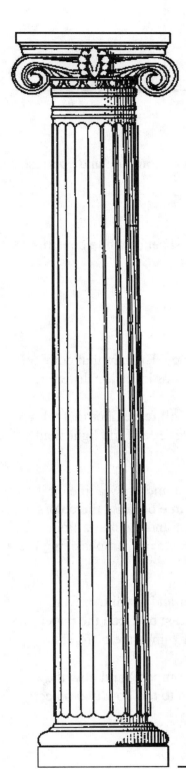

Compare & Contrast

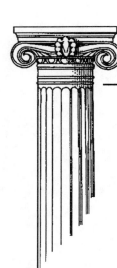

50

Objective

Students will understand the concepts and vocabulary of compare and contrast.

Materials

Sheet of black construction paper and a black crayon; sheet of white construction paper and a white crayon

Focus

Write the words "compare" and "contrast" on chalkboard or transparency. Explain that comparisons tell how two objects or ideas are alike. Contrast is how two objects or ideas are different.

1. Ask students where they have seen the word "contrast." Some will remember that televisions often have a contrast dial which makes the dark shades darker and the light shades lighter.

    To illustrate contrast, display a sheet of white construction paper and draw a line on it with a white crayon. Explain that it is difficult to see the white line because the colors are so much alike. There is very little contrast between the paper and the mark. Follow the same procedure with the black construction paper and black crayon, emphasizing the concept of contrast.

    Now make a black crayon mark on the white construction paper and a white crayon mark on the black paper to illustrate how the difference or contrast between the paper and the mark make it much easier to see. Contrast refers to how things are different.

2. Tell students that compositions can tell how objects are alike (compare) and how they are different (contrast). The prompt is usually a simple direction to tell how two objects are alike and how they are different.

3. Ask students to copy the following vocabulary list of comparison words on page 15 in Writer Reference. Encourage students to consult this list to provide variety in their comparison sentences. Define words as student needs dictate. Use the words as appropriate during the remaining lessons to familiarize the students with the subtle meanings of the words.

likewise	similar	equal	equivalent
comparable	resemble	related	much alike
much the same	complementary	in accord	analogous
akin	identical		

4. Ask students to copy the following contrast vocabulary words on page 15 in Writer Reference. Encourage students to consult this list to provide variety in their contrast sentences.

distinctive	otherwise	dissimilar	contrary
diverse	opposite	separate	particular differences
peculiar	vary	individual	inconsistent

Note: Third grade and some fourth grade students may find these vocabulary words overwhelming. Omit this part of the lesson according to the needs of the students.

Close

Review the concepts of compare and contrast by displaying the construction paper lines. Review the vocabulary words and explain that these words will keep compositions from being repetitive.

A possible assignment could be to locate the vocabulary words in a dictionary and write the definitions.

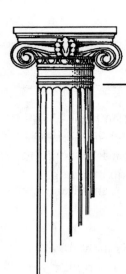

51

Objective

Students will organize information for a compare/contrast composition.

Materials

Two objects or pictures of two objects which are related but different such as pencil and pen, socks and shoes, stapler and tape dispenser, paper towel and tissue, desk and chair, hardback book and paperback book, cracker and cookie, photograph and illustration, notebook paper and white duplicating paper, dog and cat, sheep and pig, magazine and newspaper, cup and glass, hat and gloves, boots and shoes, apple and orange, banana and grapefruit, carrot and celery, broccoli and cauliflower, toothpaste and toothbrush, spoon and fork, plate and bowl, lunch sack and grocery sack, etc.; Writer Reference

Focus

As a class, reread the vocabulary lists on page 15 of Writer Reference. Encourage student use of these words as the composition develops.

1. On the chalkboard or transparency, draw a vertical line down the center. Label one side "ways to compare" and the other side "ways to contrast."

2. Display one set of objects from the materials list. Using a brainstorming technique, have students list ways the objects compare and ways they contrast.

Note: Encourage students to brainstorm at least six comparisons and six contrasts, as the first ideas are often obvious and simplistic. Later items on the lists usually provide more interesting ideas to develop for the composition.

3. Evaluate the lists and determine the three most important or most interesting comparisons and the three most important or most interesting contrasts. Place stars beside the three choices on each list. Sample lists for an apple and an orange might include the following:

Ways to compare	Ways to contrast
edible	color
*fruits	*texture
size	*peel
*seeds	pulp
*grow on trees	how cooked
juicy	*nutrition

Note: Three fully elaborated comparisons and contrasts will result in a better composition than one which has many points but lacks elaboration. In addition, often students find later that one of their choices is difficult to elaborate. In that case, the student can check the original list for a substitution.

4. Explain that when writing compare/contrast compositions, balanced treatment should be given to the likenesses and differences.

5. In small groups or pairs, ask students to repeat this activity with other pairs of objects. Ask students to share their lists with the class.

Close

Review the definitions of compare and contrast. Remind students that compositions should include equal numbers of comparisons and contrasts to make a balanced article. A homework assignment could ask students to make a list of at least six comparisons and six contrasts for two objects or pictures of objects in their homes.

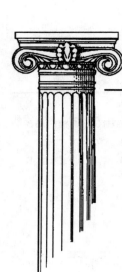

52

Objective

Students will write the introduction of a compare/contrast composition.

Materials

New examples of objects from previous lesson; chart paper or transparencies

Focus

Share homework or review the concepts of compare and contrast and the importance of having a balance of ideas for each. Display pairs of objects and state simple prompts for a compare/contrast writing assignment. For example:

- A shoe and a sock are alike in some ways and different in some ways. Write a composition to tell how they are alike and how they are different.

- A paper towel and a tissue are alike in some ways and different in some ways. Write a composition to tell how they are alike and how they are different.

- A dog and a cat are alike in some ways and different in some ways. Write a composition to tell how they are alike and how they are different.

1. Use any pair of objects and brainstorm lists of comparisons and contrasts as in the previous lesson. Star the three that are most important on each list.

2. Explain that these compositions are introduced by simply stating the prompt and then listing the comparisons and contrasts. For example:

   An apple and an orange are alike in some ways and different in some ways. They are alike because they are fruits, they are nutritional, and they grow on trees. They are different in texture, their peels, and their nutritional value.

3. Use another pair of objects to demonstrate the introduction. For example:

   A sheep and a pig are alike in some ways and different in some ways. They are alike because they are farm animals, they are mammals, and they have tails. They are different in what they eat, their outer skin, and their sounds.

4. Ask students to write introductions for the homework assignments or the classroom lists of comparisons and contrasts written in #1 above. They may work in small groups or in pairs.

5. Ask groups to share their introductions.

Close

Review the procedure for writing an introduction: state the prompt and list the three comparisons and contrasts.

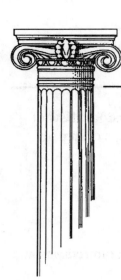

53

Objective

Students will learn the organizational outline for a compare/contrast composition.

Materials

Introductions from the previous lesson; Writer Reference; two objects for class composition; bulletin board display of compare/contrast outline (shown below)

Focus

Read an introduction from the previous lesson. Explain that the introduction tells the reader how the remaining composition will be written. Each topic mentioned in the introduction will be discussed in the same order in the composition.

1. Ask students to copy the following outline on page 16 in Writer Reference.

    Classificatory: Compare/Contrast

    Introduction
         State the prompt
         State comparisons and contrasts
    Comparisons
         First - Elaboration
         Second - Elaboration
         Third - Elaboration
    Transition sentence
    Contrasts
         First - Elaboration
         Second - Elaboration
         Third - Elaboration
    Closing
         State the prompt
         State comparisons and contrasts

2. Define elaboration as telling more detail about the topic. The elaboration can be an example, a description, or further explanation.

3. Using the two objects, ask student to brainstorm likenesses and differences for a class composition.

©ECS Learning Systems, Inc., San Antonio, TX

4. Determine the three likenesses and the three differences that will be elaborated for the composition.

5. Write an introduction for the composition.

Close

Review the outline, pointing out how the outline follows the pattern established in the introduction.

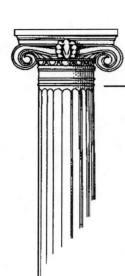

54

Objective

Students will write the body of a compare/contrast composition.

Materials

List of comparisons and contrasts and the introduction about the objects from previous lesson; chart paper or transparency; Writer Reference

Focus

Reread the list and the introduction from the previous lesson and review the outline.

1. Ask students to write the first comparison in sentence form using vocabulary from page 15 of Writer Reference. Write the sentence on a chart or transparency. For example:

   Apples and oranges are similar because they are common fruits.

2. Explain that each idea needs elaboration. The elaboration can be an example, facts, description, further explanation, or details to make the concept clear to the reader. Tell students to copy those elaboration techniques at the bottom of page 16 of Writer Reference. For example:

   There are a variety of fruits, but apples and oranges are among the favorites of many people because of their fresh, sweet tastes and their attractive appearance.

3. Continue to write and elaborate the next two comparisons in the same manner. Write the student suggestions on the chart or transparency. For example:

   Apples and oranges provide many of the same vitamins, minerals, and fiber for a healthy diet. Dietary recommendations include several servings of fruits each day, and apples and oranges fulfill those recommendations.

   Apples and oranges both grow in orchards. Oranges grow in immense groves in Florida and Texas, and apples are grown in large orchards primarily in Washington and New York.

Close

Review the organizational outline for compare/contrast compositions. Remind students that creative elaboration of each point in the outline will result in a quality composition.

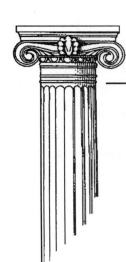

55

Objective

Students will complete the body of a compare/contrast composition.

Materials

Objects and composition from previous lesson; Writer Reference

Focus

Review the organizational outline for compare/contrast compositions. Read the composition started as a class in the previous lesson.

1. The next item on the organizational outline is "transition sentence." Ask for student suggestions about why a transition sentence is needed at this point. Answers should point out that the first topic (comparisons) needs a connection to the new topic (contrasts). The transition sentence tells the reader that the comparisons are finished and that the next part of the composition will discuss contrasts.

2. Elicit student examples of transition sentences. For example:

    While an apple and an orange resemble each other in many ways, they also have particular differences.

    Or: An apple and an orange are closely related, but they also have distinctive characteristics.

3. Ask students to write and elaborate the three contrasts in the same manner as the comparisons, paying particular attention to the vocabulary on page 15 of Writer Reference. For example:

    The outer peels of apples and oranges have particular differences. Oranges have thick, rough inedible orange-colored peels that can be removed with fingers. In contrast, apples have thin, shiny red or green peels that can be eaten or removed with a knife.

    The edible parts of apples and oranges have different characteristics. Apples have a whitish, crunchy flesh with a hard core of dark seeds in the center. Oranges have approximately ten individual sections which can be separated. Each section is filled with juice and pulp.

Apples and oranges are used in diverse ways. Oranges are usually eaten fresh and cold, and only rarely added to recipes. On the other hand, while apples are eaten fresh, they are also a part of hundreds of interesting recipes including salads, pies, cobblers, cakes, and popovers.

Close

Reread the class composition. Review the organizational strategy.

©ECS Learning Systems, Inc., San Antonio, TX

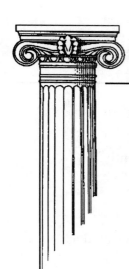

56

Objective

Students will write the conclusion and revise and edit a compare/contrast composition.

Materials

Class composition from previous lessons; student copies of compare/contrast checklist, page 134 of Appendix

Focus

Reread the class composition from the previous lessons. Review the organizational outline.

1. Explain that the ending for a compare/contrast composition is nearly identical to the introduction:

    • Restate the prompt.
    • Restate the comparisons and contrasts.
    • Optional—a personal reflection about the items.

2. Elicit student suggestions for the conclusion and write them on the chart or transparency. For example:

    Apples and oranges are alike in many ways and different in many ways. They are analogous in that they are common fruits, they contribute to healthy diets, and they grow in orchards. Apples and oranges are dissimilar in their peels, flesh, and uses. Most people enjoy eating both of these delicious fruits.

3. Using the compare/contrast checklist, revise and edit the composition. Pay particular attention to the compare and contrast vocabulary. The checklist can be modified to meet the needs of the students.

Close

Reread the entire composition. Point out the organizational outline as the composition is read. As a homework assignment, ask students to select two objects to be the subject of a compare/contrast composition.

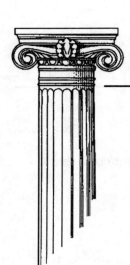

57

Objective

Students will write a compare/contrast composition independently.

Materials

Writer Reference, objects for topics from lesson 51 or topics selected as homework

Focus

Review the steps in writing a compare/contrast composition:

1. Make a list of six ways the objects or ideas are alike.
2. Make a list of six ways the objects or ideas are different.
3. Select the three best ideas from each list.
4. Follow the outline.

Instruct students to write a compare/contrast composition using the techniques and processes learned.

Be sure each student follows the process and uses the checklist to revise and edit.

Give students an opportunity to share their compositions with others.

Date and save compositions in students' portfolios.

Close

Comment positively about the writing skills students have acquired.

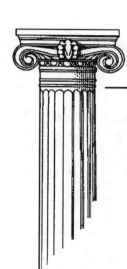

58

Objective

Students will write compositions about the advantages and disadvantages of a task or an idea.

Materials

Writer Reference, bulletin board display of vocabulary words:

Advantages	**Disadvantages**
superiority	handicap
upper hand	inconvenience
edge	hindrance
head start	unfavorable
fitness	unprofitable
relevance	damaging
usefulness	hurtful
betterment	detrimental
improvement	inconvenient
worthwhile	drawback
favorable	disability
instrumental	obstacle
pleasing	displeasing

Note: Third grade and some fourth grade students may find these vocabulary words overwhelming. Omit the vocabulary part of this lesson accoring to the needs of the students. Younger students may also benefit from using the simple terms of "good" and "bad" in place of "advantage" and "disadvantage."

Focus

Explain that advantage/disadvantage compositions use the same outline and writing process as compare/contrast compositions.

1. Share some examples of advantage/disadvantage writing topics, such as:

   buying lunch in the cafeteria
   saving money
   being the oldest (or youngest or middle) child in the family
   living in a city (or farm or small town)
   being in a certain grade in school
   summer
   winter

2. Add the word "Advantage" beside "Compare" on the bulletin board outline for compare/contrast. Direct students to add the word to their outline in Writer Reference on page 16.

3. Add the word "Disadvantage" beside "Contrasts" on the bulletin board outline. Direct students to add the word to their outline in Writer Reference on page 16.

4. Point out that particular vocabulary words will improve advantage/disadvantage compositions. Direct students to copy the vocabulary words from the bulletin board display to page 17 of Writer Reference.

5. Select one of the topics in #1 above as a class composition. With student suggestions, develop six advantages and six disadvantages in the same manner as compare/contrast compositions. Determine three advantages and three disadvantages to develop in the composition.

6. Assign each one of the advantages and disadvantages to small groups of students. Direct each group to fully develop the advantages and disadvantages, paying particular attention to vocabulary.

7. Caution students to avoid advantages such as, "It's fun!" or "It's good!" or "It's neat." These concepts are difficult to elaborate.

8. Quickly order and read the advantages and disadvantages produced by the groups.

Close

Remind students that advantage/disadvantage compositions are written in the same format as compare/contrast compositions. The only differences to note involve the vocabulary.

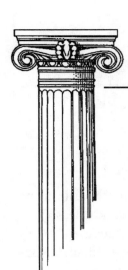

59

Objective

Students will write an advantage/disadvantage composition independently.

Materials

Writer Reference

Focus

Review the steps in writing an advantage/disadvantage composition:

1. Make a list of six advantages.
2. Make a list of six disadvantages.
3. Select the three best ideas from each list.
4. Follow the outline.

Instruct students to write an advantage/disadvantage composition using the techniques and processes learned.

Be sure each student follows the process and uses the checklist to revise and edit.

Provide students an opportunity to share their compositions with others.

Close

Comment positively about the writing skills the students have acquired.

60

Objective

Putting it all together:

Provide opportunities for students to write one compare/contrast composition and one advantage/disadvantage composition before proceeding to the next lessons. Students typically find this writing relatively easy to accomplish because it requires fairly close adherence to the outline. Creativity is expressed in the ideas on the planning lists, the elaboration, the use of words, and sentence choices.

Use the checklist to establish areas for reteaching, and expect improvement on subsequent compositions.

Never skip the sharing of compositions. This part of the writing process provides immeasurable motivation to young writers.

Date and save compositions in students' portfolios.

For students who will be evaluated on a standardized writing test, provide writing prompts for this topic that are consistent with the testing format. Students find it difficult to fully demonstrate their writing skills if they are not familiar with the format.

©ECS Learning Systems, Inc., San Antonio, TX

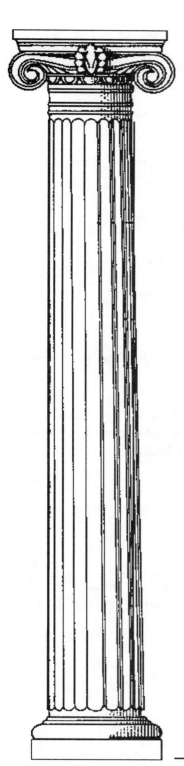

Persuasion

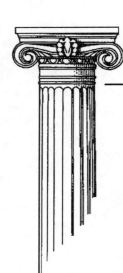

61

Objective

Students will review four forms of writing: description, narration, direction, and compare/contrast.

Materials

Writer Reference; bulletin board displays of writing concepts

Focus

Ask students to list the four types of writing they have learned thus far. On chalkboard or transparency, list headings for each type.

1. Ask students to recall major concepts related to descriptive writing. Students should refer to information collected in Writer Reference as they review the concepts. List their responses on the chalkboard or transparency. Key points should include the organizational strategy and the importance of elaboration.

2. Continue with a similar review of each of the remaining three types of writing.

Close

Point out the common themes throughout the four kinds of writing, particularly organizational strategy and elaboration. Compliment students on the skills they have acquired thus far. Explain that they are now ready to learn a fifth type of writing called persuasion.

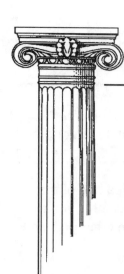

62

Objective

Students will understand the premise of persuasive writing.

Materials

Magazine, newspaper, or bulk mail advertisements that illustrate the role of persuasion (try to include some that are narrative in style); magazine articles that are a plea for action or change in opinion; editorials or letters to the editor of a magazine or newspaper that illustrate persuasive writing

Focus

Share some advertisements, articles, and editorials as examples of persuasion. Define persuasion as winning over someone to your way of thinking. Emphasize that persuasive writing is a critical part of a democracy where people have the right to express their ideas. Most people have a need to persuade others to their ideas at some point in their lives. For example, persuasive writing plays a key role in businesses who need to let customers know of their services or products. Students use persuasion to convince their parents to let them do something or buy something.

1. Ask students to share some events in which they persuaded their parents to let them do something or buy something. Ask them to identify the reasons why their parents changed their minds about an issue.

2. Explain that good persuasive thinking and writing helps convince others to agree with your ideas.

3. Read some examples of persuasive writing topics:

   • Think of one rule in your classroom that you would like to change. Write a letter in which you tell your teacher what the rule is and try to convince your teacher to change it.

   • Many people think that children and adults watch too much television. What is your opinion on this issue? Write a letter to the editor of your newspaper in which you state your position and provide convincing reasons for your belief.

   • Your parents are considering giving you an allowance instead of giving you money whenever you need it. Which would you rather have? Write a letter to your parents explaining your position, and give good reasons for your belief.

- Your teacher is considering the merits of giving homework every day. What is your opinion of daily homework? Write a letter to your teacher in which you state your opinion and give reasons for your position.

- A neighbor's pig gave birth to a litter of piglets. The mother pig abandoned one of the piglets. Write a letter to your family explaining why it would be a good idea for you to take care of the piglet for a few weeks until it can go back to live with the other pigs and survive.

- Many people think that television shows have too much violence in them. What is your opinion? Write a letter to a television station stating your opinion and giving good reasons for your belief.

- The school board is considering a pilot year-round school. Students would attend school the same number of days, but would have a two-week vacation after every six weeks of school rather than a three-month summer vacation. Write a letter to the school board expressing your opinion either for or against this idea.

- Some people think we should change the school mascot. What do you think? Write a letter to the principal explaining why you think this is a good or a bad idea. Give convincing reasons for your choice.

- Your parents are considering letting you have a pet (an animal of your choice). Write a letter to your parents explaining why getting a pet is a good idea. Give good reasons for having that pet.

- Some parents pay their children for getting good grades on their report cards. Do you think this is a good idea? Write a letter to your parents explaining your position and give reasons for your ideas.

- In some schools, all students wear uniforms. Do you think this is a good idea? Write a letter to the principal explaining your opinion and giving reasons for your view.

- You would really like a certain item for your birthday. Write a letter to your parents explaining why you should have that item. Give convincing reasons for your opinion.

- You have read a great book. You think other students would really enjoy reading the same book. Write a letter to a friend explaining why (s)he should read this particular book.

- Your parents want your opinions on where they should take a vacation. Write a letter to your parents explaining where you would like to go on vacation and give convincing reasons why yours is the best choice.

- Your parents cook a certain food that you particularly like. Write a letter to your parents explaining why they should serve that food at your birthday party. Give reasons for wanting that food served.

- Your friends are trying to decide whether to go to a movie or go on a picnic in the park. Which would you rather do? Write a letter to your friends telling them which you would rather do. Give convincing reasons for your choice.

- Your principal is considering whether or not your school should have a snack bar. She has asked students for their opinions. Write a letter to your principal in which you state your position and provide convincing reasons for your belief.

4. Point out that much persuasive writing is written to a specific person or audience in letter form.

Close

Point out that persuasive writing is an important part of our country. For a homework assignment, ask students to bring an example of persuasive writing (advertisement, editorial, etc.) and a possible topic for persuasive writing.

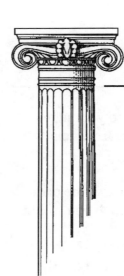

63

Objective

Students will develop information for persuasive writing.

Materials

Persuasive materials from previous lesson; homework assignments; Writer Reference; list of persuasive prompts from previous lesson written on chart paper or transparencies; chart paper or transparency

Focus

Review the definition of persuasive writing and its importance in daily life. Display some persuasive materials from previous lesson. Discuss how effective persuasive writing can be an important tool in accomplishing personal goals.

1. Share homework assignments. Identify those writing topics that might make good persuasive prompts and write them on a chart or transparency for later reference.

2. Display the list of writing prompts from the previous lesson and also the prompts provided in the student homework. As a class, select a prompt to be the topic of a class composition. Be sure the topic has nearly universal support from the students so that some will not be alienated by the topic.

Note: The writing prompt used for teacher example in these lessons is as follows:

- Your principal is considering whether or not your school should have a snack bar. She has asked students for their opinions. Write a letter to your principal in which you state your position and provide convincing reasons for your belief.

3. Brainstorm a list of at least ten reasons that could be used in the composition. As with compare/contrast compositions, the first ideas suggested may not be the best ideas. A long list of ideas requires students to explore many possibilities. Write the list on a chart or transparency. For example:

food would look better in the snack bar
different foods could be available
fewer workers needed
available for recess or breaks during day
supplement lunch

make extra profit for school
first school in district to have one
get to select food
parents would enjoy choices
older students already have it

4. Ask students to select the three best reasons for use in a class composition. Those three reasons should then be ranked in order of importance, beginning with the least important and progressing to the most important.

Note: While there are other valid organizational strategies for persuasive writing, this form works well for most situations, and young writers seem to understand the reasoning.

5. Discuss the strategy for listing the most important reason last. The reader will probably best remember the last one read, so it makes sense to end the composition with the strongest point.

Note: Student compositions need not be limited to three reasons, but three should be presented as a minimum number to be included in a composition, particularly for younger students. Older students can reasonably be expected to include more than three. A far better composition results when a few reasons are fully developed than when a long list of reasons is presented with little elaboration of each issue.

Close

Explain that developing a list of reasons for a certain argument is the first step to writing a good persuasive composition. A long list of reasons allows the writer to select the best ideas to be included in the composition.

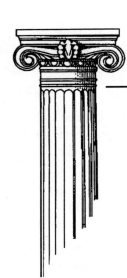

64

Objective

Students will learn an organizational strategy for persuasive writing.

Materials

List of persuasive reasons generated in previous lesson; chart paper or transparency; Writer Reference; bulletin board display of persuasive outline:

> Introduction
> > Statement of issue
> > Statement of opinion
> > Tell sources of information
> > Request reader to consider ideas
> Reason 1 - elaboration
> Reason 2 - elaboration
> Reason 3 - elaboration
> Conclusion
> > Restate opinion
> > Compliment reader
> > Request reader to consider ideas

Focus

Remind students of the importance of persuasive writing. Review the writing prompt selected in the previous lesson, and reread the persuasive reasons generated for the class composition.

1. Ask students to determine logical information to include in the introduction to persuasive writing. Answers should include a statement of the issue to be discussed. Explain that the issue to be discussed can be written directly from the prompt.

2. Tell students that in addition to the statement of the issue, introductions to persuasive writing include several other important parts that are different from introductions they have learned for other forms of writing. Refer to the bulletin board display to discuss each of the parts of the introduction.

3. Using the topic the class selected, write an introduction to the composition. The statement of the issue comes directly from the prompt. Be sure to include the four parts of the introduction. Write the introduction on a chart or transparency. For example:

You are considering having a snack bar at our school. Our opinion is that we should have a snack bar. In class discussions, we have considered reasons for having a snack bar. We hope that you agree that our ideas are worthy of your consideration.

4. Ask students to copy the persuasive writing introduction and remaining outline on page 18 of Writer Reference. This outline will serve as a guide for independent compositions.

Close

Review the outline of persuasive compositions. Future lessons will explain how to do each part of the composition.

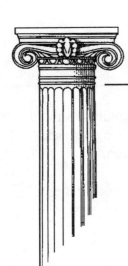

65

Objective

Students will participate in writing a whole class persuasive composition.

Materials

Writer Reference; a bulletin board display of the following information:

> Persuasive elaboration:
> facts about the issue
> reasons for importance
> comparisons
> examples
> details

Focus

Review the persuasive writing outline. Show how the organizational strategy will help the reader understand and make sense of the composition.

1. Reread the introduction from the previous lesson. Begin a new paragraph to continue developing the composition as a class. Ask students to explain the reason for indenting a new paragraph at this point in the composition. Answers should reflect the fact that the introduction is completed and the first paragraph of the body should be indented.

2. The first reason should be stated at the beginning of the paragraph. For example:

   > We think that a snack bar would be very convenient and helpful during recess and breaks during our school day.

3. Tell students that each reason needs to be fully elaborated so that the reader will understand all aspects of the reason. Post the following elaboration topics on a bulletin board display:

   > facts about the issue
   > reasons for importance
   > comparisons
   > examples
   > details

   Ask students to list these five items at the bottom of page 18 of Writer Reference where they have written the persuasive outline.

　©ECS Learning Systems, Inc., San Antonio, TX

4. Tell students that some key words can be helpful in persuasive writing. Write the following words on chart paper or transparency for future reference. Select those words that are most appropriate to the class and/or grade level. Ask students to copy the list on page 19 of Writer Reference.

important issue	important to note
for this reason	especially important
noteworthy	the basic idea
to emphasize	a distinctive concept
central idea	above all else
key feature	in face of this issue
most of all	particularly relevant
the main value	more than anything else
truly	particularly important
significant factor	particularly valuable

Note: Third grade and some fourth grade students may find these vocabulary words overwhelming. Omit this part of the lesson according to the needs of the students.

5. Write elaboration for the first reason. For example:

Students get hungry in the morning, and when students are hungry, their stomachs growl. Such annoying growling could be a significant factor in disturbing a class. Other students become irritable and unable to concentrate when they are hungry. Clearly, school achievement suffers when students do not have the opportunity to have a snack. A snack bar would be a helpful solution to the problem of hungry students.

Close

Review the process for writing a persuasive composition. Reread the composition as it has been written, pointing out the organizational strategy. Relate the writing to the persuasive outline, explaining that the composition will be completed in the next lesson. Emphasize the importance of fully elaborating each reason.

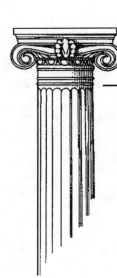

66

Objective

Students will complete a class persuasive composition.

Materials

Writer Reference; composition in progress from previous lesson

Focus

Review the persuasive outline and the vocabulary for developing persuasive compositions. Reread the composition initiated in the previous lesson.

1. Ask students to develop elaboration for the second and third reasons they listed previously for this composition. Copy their responses on the chart or transparency.

2. Ask students to refer to the persuasive outline for information to be included in the conclusion. Ask students to generate a conclusion which includes the required information.

    -   The first statement in the conclusion is a restatement of the issue and the writer's opinion.
    -   A second statement is a compliment to the reader, possibly pointing out past decisions which were important or positive.
    -   A last sentence should be a hope that the reader will agree with the writer.

3. Reread the entire class composition.

Close

Review the importance of persuasive writing. Point out how this whole class composition follows the persuasive outline. Explain that the next lesson will be devoted to revising and editing the composition.

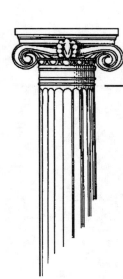

67

Objective

Students will revise and edit a class persuasive composition.

Materials

Class composition from previous lesson; student copies of persuasive writing checklist from page 135 of the Appendix

Focus

Quickly reread the composition from the previous lesson.

1. Remind students that revision and editing of persuasive compositions is similar to previous types of writing. The key issues of quality remain organization, full development of the topic, and rich vocabulary.

2. Ask students to revise and edit the composition using the writing checklist. The checklist can be revised and adapted to meet the needs of the students.

Close

Read the final copy of the composition. Compliment students on the quality of the work. As a possible homework assignment, ask each student to select a topic for an individual persuasive composition.

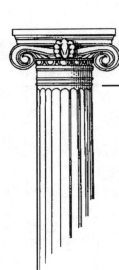

68

Objective

Putting it all together:

Using Writer Reference and bulletin board displays, review the persuasive writing outline. Explain that each student is now capable of writing a persuasive composition.

Students should follow the procedure below to write a persuasive composition:

1. List nine or ten reasons for the idea
2. Select the three best reasons
3. Rank the reasons from least important to most important
4. Follow the outline
5. Revise and edit
6. Publish
7. Share

Never skip the sharing process because it provides powerful motivation for writing. The class time invested in sharing work is time well spent.

Ask students to place persuasive compositions in their portfolios. Compare and contrast these compositions to earlier writing.

Students have made significant progress in writing skills, and a review of their lessons will demonstrate how much they have learned.

They should note that major similarities exist in all five types of writing: clear organization, elaboration, rich vocabulary, and complex sentence structure.

Provide a variety of prompts from all five types of writing and allow students to select topics for their compositions.

Students who are being tested should be offered a variety of prompts consistent with the testing format. Students should be able to identify which kind of writing would best suit the requirements of the testing prompts.

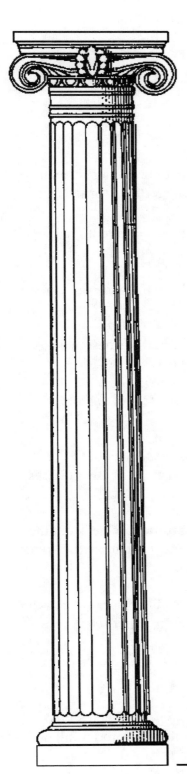

Appendix

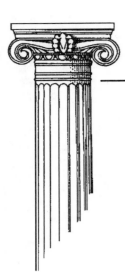

Suggestions for Sharing Written Work

Regular sharing of writing skills is extremely important in keeping students motivated to communicate. Below are some further suggestions for sharing:

1. Read compositions to other classes, on the same or different grade levels.

2. Copy a set of compositions and bind them. Check the book out to the students to share at home.

3. Place a copy of the compositions in the library. Perhaps design a display that will draw attention to the students' work.

4. Place a copy of the compositions in the office for school visitors to read.

5. Ask students to tape record their compositions. Several could be recorded on one tape. Present the tape to the library and to other classes who can listen at their convenience.

6. Videotape the students as they read their compositions. Check out the videotape to the students so they can take it home to share with parents and friends. Place a copy in the school library.

7. As often as possible, display compositions in visible places such as the classroom, hallway, cafeteria, library, gymnasium, office, etc.

8. Put compositions in classroom "library." Allow students to "check out" the compositions with library cards.

9. Plan an authors' party. Invite parents and school personnel to come. Let students create invitations and plan refreshments. A room full of colored balloons creates a quick and festive party mood. Display student compositions, and allow each student to select one favorite composition to read at the party. This is a great opportunity to showcase students' writing and reward their efforts.

10. A portable, adjustable music stand makes an excellent podium.

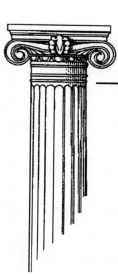

Suggested Topics for Lesson 2

The best topics are integrated with other activities the students are learning. Science, social studies, math, and literature units provide excellent sources of mini topics for this lesson. The students are motivated to write if they help select their own topics. For example, if students are studying frogs, some mini topics for this lesson might be:

> what frogs look like
> what frogs eat
> where frogs live
> how frogs grow
> difference between frogs and toads
> why you like frogs
> why you don't like frogs
> tell what happens in the story "The Frog Prince" or any other story
> tell the main characters in "The Frog Prince" or any other story
> tell your opinion of "The Frog Prince" or any other story

Be particularly sensitive to the topics selected. The ideas will be developed as a class, but be sure that all students understand and relate to the topics. Do not use this activity as a test of their knowledge, but use it rather to illustrate how writing communicates ideas.

For students who finish the daily class story early, encourage them to select a topic of their own, and write a short story. Or, the following topics might be used for further ideas. Most are topics that all students can understand. For convenience, this list could be posted in the room for easy reference. Most students will not need an extra topic each day, as they will be busy with the standard assignment. For those who do manage an extra story, be sure to reward their efforts to encourage them to continue their writing.

desks	chairs	specific books
tables	paper	pencils
glue	scissors	rubber bands
chalkboard	eraser	library
cafeteria	office	playground
weather	food items	specific toys
specific animals	shoes	trucks
eyes	fingers	feet
trees	water	beds

Look at the picture. Describe what you see.

Look at the picture. Describe what you see.

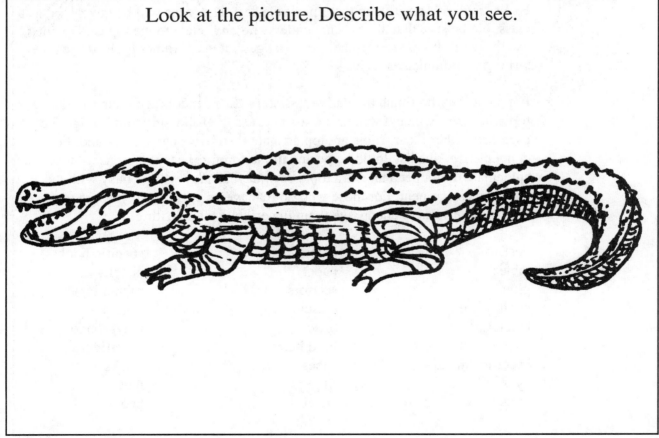

Look at the picture. Describe what you see.

Name

_____

Descriptions

In your composition, you have:

___ followed directions

___ correct order

___ sequence words - blue

___ three sentences about each item

___ expanded, complex sentences

___ long composition

___ location words - red

___ similes using *as* - green

___ similes using *like* - yellow

___ star writer words - stars

___ purposes for objects/actions

___ sensory details - purple

___ interesting words - orange

___ most words spelled correctly

___ correct punctuation

___ complete sentences

___ correct tense

___ neat handwriting

Name

_____

Stories

In your composition, you have:

___ followed directions

___ a clear beginning

___ a clear conclusion

___ correct order

___ sequence words - blue

___ expanded, complex sentences

___ fully developed ideas

___ long composition

___ location words - red

___ similes (*as* and *like*) - green, yellow

___ star writer words - stars

___ sensory details - purple

___ interesting verbs - orange

___ most words spelled correctly

___ correct punctuation

___ complete sentences

___ correct tense

___ neat handwriting

Story Introductions				
Book Title	Kind of Day	Time	Site	Action

Name

_____

Directions

In your composition, you have:

___ followed directions

___ a clear introduction

___ a clear conclusion

___ correct order

___ sequence words - blue

___ expanded, complex sentences

___ long composition

___ location words - red

___ star writer words - stars

___ elaboration with details

___ elaboration with examples

___ elaboration with reasons

___ interesting words - orange

___ most words spelled correctly

___ correct punctuation

___ complete sentences

___ correct tense

___ neat handwriting

Name

_____

Compare/Contrast

In your composition, you have:

___ followed directions

___ a clear introduction

___ a clear conclusion

___ correct order

___ sequence words - blue

___ expanded, complex sentences

___ long composition

___ location words - red

___ star writer words - stars

___ elaboration with details

___ elaboration with examples

___ elaboration with reasons

___ interesting words - orange

___ most words spelled correctly

___ correct punctuation

___ complete sentences

___ correct tense

___ neat handwriting

Name

_____

Persuasion

In your composition, you have:

___ followed directions

___ a clear introduction

___ a clear conclusion

___ correct order

___ sequence words - blue

___ expanded, complex sentences

___ long composition

___ star writer words - stars

___ elaboration with facts

___ elaboration with reasons

___ elaboration with comparisons

___ elaboration with examples

___ persuasive vocabulary

___ interesting words

___ most words spelled correctly

___ correct punctuation

___ complete sentences

___ correct tense

___ neat handwriting

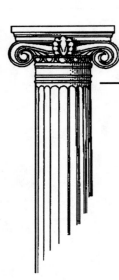

Index of Lesson Objectives

Writing Process
1 Develop topics for compositions
2 Learn writing routines
3 Edit
4 Writer Reference for spelling help
5 Write using routines
6 Prewriting
7 Writing
8 Edit
9 Rewrite to publish
10 Share

Writing Skills
11 Recognize similes
12 Create similes
13 Interesting words
14 Word bank, thesaurus
15 Interesting verbs
16 Write sensory adjectives as a class
17 Write sensory adjectives as individuals
18 Create sensory sentences
19 Expand and rearrange sentences
20 Practice sentence expansion
21 Write a composition

Descriptions
22 Organize descriptions
23 Sequence words
24 Location words
25 Action
26 Whole class writing
27 Editing checklist and color code
28 Independent compositions
29 Putting it all together

Narratives
30 Qualities of narrative prompts
31 Qualities of introductions
32 Kind of day

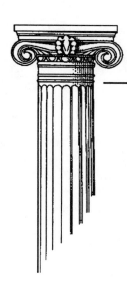

Directions

Compare/Contrast

Persuasion

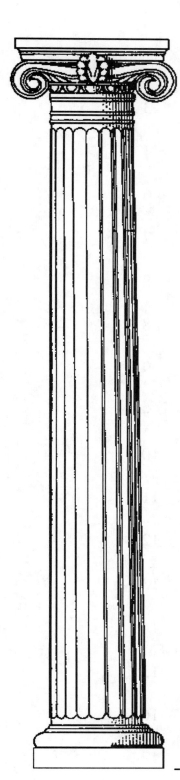

Writer
Reference

Table of Contents

Similes

1. as funny as a monkey
2. as hard as a rock
3. as easy as pie
4. as hot as fire
5. as black as ink
6. as funny as a clown
7. as cold as ice
8. as soft as a cloud
9. as pretty as a picture
10. as sharp as a tack
11. as big as a house
12. as smelly as a skunk
13. as wiggly as a worm
14. as blue as the sky
15. as hungry as a horse
16. as sweet as sugar
17. as happy as a clown
18. as sour as a lemon
19. as white as a sheet
20. as red as a rose
21. as yellow as the sun
22. as fast as lightning
23. as tall as a building
24. as loud as thunder
25. as fat as a pig
26. as slippery as an eel
27. as green as grass
28. as slow as a turtle
29. as smooth as glass
30. as good as gold

Word Bank

bad   _____   _____   _____

big   _____   _____   _____

boy   _____   _____   _____

cold   _____   _____   _____

cry   _____   _____   _____

eat   _____   _____   _____

fat   _____   _____   _____

friend   _____   _____   _____

girl   _____   _____   _____

go (went)   _____   _____   _____

good   _____   _____   _____

happy   _____   _____   _____

hot   _____   _____   _____

little   _____   _____   _____

look   _____   _____   _____

4

Word Bank

many   _____   _____   _____

nice   _____   _____   _____

old   _____   _____   _____

play   _____   _____   _____

pretty   _____   _____   _____

ride   _____   _____   _____

run   _____   _____   _____

sad   _____   _____   _____

say (said)   _____   _____   _____

scare   _____   _____   _____

take   _____   _____   _____

tell   _____   _____   _____

walk   _____   _____   _____

watch   _____   _____   _____

yell   _____   _____   _____

Sensory Details Categories

Size	Shape	Touch	Smell	Sound	Taste

Expanded Sentences

_____

_____

_____

_____

_____

_____

_____

_____

6

Star Writer Words

★ _____   ★ _____

★ _____   ★ _____

★ _____   ★ _____

★ _____   ★ _____

★ _____   ★ _____

★ _____   ★ _____

★ _____   ★ _____

★ _____   ★ _____

★ _____   ★ _____

★ _____   ★ _____

★ _____   ★ _____

7

Sequence Words	Location Words

8

Kind of Day	Time

9

Sites

10

Actions

11

Story Outline with Sites

12

Story Outline with Problem

Directions Outline

©ECS Learning Systems, Inc., San Antonio, TX

Compare/Contrast Vocabulary

15

Compare/Contrast Outline

16

Advantages/Disadvantages Vocabulary

Persuasive Outline

18

Persuasive Vocabulary

Words for My Writing

About the Author

Frustrated by the lack of specific directions and detailed lesson plans for writing, Charlotte Slack developed this writing program drawing upon 25 years of teaching experience in elementary classrooms. She is currently a fourth-grade teacher in College Station, Texas. She earned her Bachelor of Science and master's degrees from the Ohio State University, and further certification at Texas A & M University. Charlotte has presented numerous workshops and has published articles in *Highlights for Children, Learning,* and *Writing Teacher* magazines. She is the author of a college textbook for preservice teachers titled *Teaching Children to Write: Theory into Practice* published by Prentice Hall.

Charlotte and Doug Slack have been married for 35 years, and have two grown daughters, Kathy and Sandy, and one grandson. Charlotte pays special thanks to her family and the many colleagues and students who encouraged her to put this writing program into book form.